Contest

ESSAYS BY CANADIAN STUDENTS

SECOND EDITION

EDITED BY
ROBERT HOOKEY
MURRAY MCARTHUR
JOAN PILZ

Contest

ESSAYS BY
CANADIAN STUDENTS

SECOND EDITION

EDITED BY
ROBERT HOOKEY
SHERIDAN COLLEGE
MURRAY MCARTHUR
UNIVERSITY OF WATERLOO
JOAN PILZ
HUMBER COLLEGE

HARCOURT
BRACE
CANADA

HARCOURT BRACE & COMPANY, CANADA
TORONTO MONTREAL ORLANDO FORT WORTH SAN DIEGO PHILADELPHIA
LONDON SYDNEY TOKYO

Requests for permission to make copies of any part of the work should be mailed to: Permissions, College Division, Harcourt Brace & Company, Canada Inc., 55 Horner Avenue, Toronto, Ontario, M8Z 4X6.

Every reasonable effort has been made to acquire permission for copyright material used in this text, and to acknowledge all such indebtedness accurately. Any errors and omissions called to the publisher's attention will be corrected in future printings.

Canadian Cataloguing in Publication Data

Main entry under title:

Contest : essays by Canadian students

2nd ed.
ISBN 0-7747-3219-9

1. English language — Rhetoric. 2. English language — Composition and exercises. 3. College prose, Canadian (English).* 4. Canadian essays (English — 20th century. I. Hookey, Robert. II. McArthur, Murray Gilchrist, 1953– . III. Pilz, Joan.

PE1417.C65 1994   808'.0427   C93-094204-3

Publisher: Heather McWhinney
Editorial and Marketing Manager: Michael J. Young
Developmental Editor: Nancy Ennis
Editorial and Marketing Co-ordinator: Kelly Picavet
Director of Publishing Services: Jean Lancee
Editorial Manager: Marcel Chiera
Production Editor: Theresa Fitzgerald
Production Manager: Sue-Ann Becker
Production Co-ordinator: Denise Wake
Copy Editor: Shaun Oakey
Interior Design: Jack Steiner Graphic Design
Cover Design: Dave Peters
Typesetting: Louisa Schulz
Typesetting and Assembly: Debbie Fleming
Printing and Binding: Hignell Printing Limited
Cover Art: L.L. FitzGerald, *Still Life with Hat*, c. 1955. Private Collection. Reproduced with the permission of Patricia and Earl Green.

This book was printed in Canada on acid-free paper.

1 2 3 4 5   98 97 96 95 94

PREFACE

In 1989, Harcourt Brace & Company held the first of its national contests for essays written by students in Canadian universities and community colleges. The contest was designed to find the best essays written by students in Canada in that year. The motivation behind the contest was the idea that students might learn a great deal about writing by reading essays produced by their peers. In essays written by classmates from across the country, students would first see reflected both their own concerns and their personal struggles with the writing process. A volume collecting exemplary essays of this sort would provide, the reasoning went, rich learning opportunities for students and teachers. Models of this sort could be used in the writing class not as masterpieces to be admired as flawless and distant paradigms, but as pieces of writing that students themselves had produced. As readers and writers, students would be on an equal footing with the models they discussed, admired, and emulated.

The winners of this contest, selected by judges from universities and colleges across the country, were published as *Contest: Essays by Canadian Students*. This second edition aims to build upon the enormous success of the first volume. Collected in this edition are the ten winners of the second national contest held in 1992, sixteen of the original winners, and ten professional models. This second edition carries forward the original motivation of providing a text for peer analysis and emulation, while adding the complementary possibilities of the analysis, discussion, and emulation of professional models. In this volume, students can see essays written by their peers alongside essays written by professionals, by other people who also have been involved in the writing process. Publishing contest winners and professionals together will perhaps bridge the gap between student aspiration and the rich treasury of traditional and contemporary writing.

The second Harcourt Brace student essay contest was held in the fall of 1992. The hundreds of submissions from across the country were evaluated and ranked by teams of judges, and the final decisions were made by the editor. Although many other essays were more than worthy of inclusion, only one winner was selected for each of the rhetorical modes that organize the volume. The winners of the 1992 Harcourt Brace student essay contest are as follows:

Description
Robert Newman
The View from the Businessman's Corner Window
Instructor: Philip Allingham
University of British Columbia

Narration
Dawn Strathy
Incarnacion
Instructor: Gisela Nolting
Concordia University

Example
Elke Bittmann
Is Happiness Only a State of Mind?
Instructor: D. Bridge
Mount Royal College

Process
Patricia Schmida
Self-Analysis Through Dream Exploration
Instructor: Deborah Bowen
University of Ottawa

Definition
Patrick Riley
Anyphone
Instructor: Tom McKendy
Marianopolis College

Classification
Laura J. Turner
Truth or Consequences
Instructor: B. Powell
University of Regina

Comparison and Contrast
George Duff
Co-operative Games
Instructor: C.A. Silber
University of Toronto

Analogy
Clint Saulteaux
Parallel Plains
Instructor: Brenda Macdonald Riches
Saskatchewan Indian Federated College

Cause and Effect
Wayne Atkinson
Death: A Warning for the Living
Instructor: Linda Early
Cariboo College

Argument
Gizelle Popradi
Post–Saturday Morning Revelations
Instructor: Tom McKendy
Marianopolis College

The winners and their instructors are to be congratulated on such excellent work.

Of the thirty-six original essays, sixteen were selected for inclusion in this volume to provide continuity with the first edition. The essays were chosen solely for their suitability and for balance of representation with the ten winners of the second contest and the ten professional models. In future editions of *Contest: Essays by Canadian Students* any of the original thirty-six may be selected for the same reasons. Sixteen were chosen so that the number of essays would be consistent with the first volume and provide the teacher and student with the same wide range of choice and opportunity.

The ten professional models included are as follows:

Description
Margaret Laurence, *The Shack*

Narration
Carol Geddes, *Growing Up Native*

Example
Erika Ritter, *Bicycles*

Process
Donald M. Murray, *The Maker's Eye: Revising Your Own Manuscripts*

Definition
Neil Bissoondath, *I'm Not Racist But ...*

Classification
Robertson Davies, *A Few Kind Words for Superstition*

Comparison and Contrast
Anna Quindlen, *The Knight and the Jester*

Analogy
Annie Dillard, *Untying the Knot*

Cause and Effect
Michele Landsberg, *Ceremonies*

Argument
Ken Dryden, *The Game*

The models were chosen in the interests of providing a primarily but not exclusively Canadian perspective. They were also chosen to represent, as much as possible, the balance and range of perspectives in Canadian history and life. With only ten places restricted to ten rhetorical modes, not everyone could be included. Any inadvertent exclusions will, we hope, be rectified in future editions.

Above all, this volume is designed to encourage students in the discipline and pleasures of writing, in the process and practice of written communication. As Patricia Schmida observed, "In writing this essay, I learned that to write what interests me is actually the best way to write what interests other people. I learned to trust my own voice." So many of our winners report on the discipline required to produce their essay. Robert Newman observed that he "learned how to have the patience to rewrite draft after draft without giving up." But they also reported on the knowledge gained, on the pleasure the discipline produced. Wayne Atkinson noted, "While writing this essay, I was forced to sort out my feelings toward life and what my priorities in life were. However, I found the writing process to be very therapeutic and have used writing to help sort out other problems and frustrations as well." All of the winners also reported an experience much like Clint Saulteaux's: "My writing developed as I started discovering who I really was. I believe that all individuals on this planet have a gift of individuality, something to offer someone and everyone else." This volume contains many of these gifts.

Acknowledgements

I would like to take this opportunity to express my gratitude to Bob Hookey, who first proposed the project to Harcourt Brace & Company, Canada, and who laid the groundwork for the text accompanying the essays; to the following reviewers, chosen by Harcourt Brace & Company, Canada, for their valuable comments: Reid Gilbert, Carol McCandless, and Jack Robinson; to my editors at Harcourt Brace & Company, Canada, Michael Young, Nancy Ennis, and Theresa Fitzgerald for their wonderful support, encouragement, and assistance. Thanks also to Kelly Picavet for her help with the manuscript.

On behalf of Harcourt Brace & Company, Canada, I would like to thank the judges who gave so generously of their time. The judges for the 1992 contest were the following:

Deb Bridges
Mount Royal College

Hal Burnham
Algonquin College

Dan Foster
Red Deer College

Bernie Gaidosch
George Brown College

Reid Gilbert
Capilano College

Anita Hurwitz
University of Windsor

Ken Long
University of Windsor

Carol McCandless
Capilano College

Sheila Page
University of Winnipeg

Brenda Riches
University of Regina

Jack Robinson
Grant MacEwan College

Ritva Seppanon
Concordia University

Maureen Shawn
Kwantlen College

Derek Soles
Camosun College

David Southmayd
Vanier College

Jim Streeter
Seneca College

Brian Turner
University of Winnipeg

We are grateful for the support and encouragement of our colleagues across the country.

Above all, I have to thank my wife, Kathryn, for her invaluable advice, her patient assistance, and the important contributions she made to this volume. I will remember always our editorial sessions in our little house on that mountain in France. Special thanks also to our daughters, Rachel and Caitlin, for allowing their parents to get on with their work and for showing us again the fun of writing.

Murray McArthur
University of Waterloo

A Note from the Publisher
Thank you for selecting *Contest: Essays by Canadian Students*, Second Edition, edited by Robert Hookey, Murray McArthur, and Joan Pilz. The editors and publishers have devoted considerable time to the careful development of this book. We appreciate your recognition of this effort and accomplishment.

We want to hear what you think about *Contest: Essays by Canadian Students*, Second Edition. Please take a few minutes to fill in the stamped reply card that you will find at the back of the book. Your comments, suggestions, and criticisms will be valuable to us as we prepare new editions and other books.

CONTENTS

PART 1: The Writing Process 1

PART 2: Expressive Writing 19

PART 3: Expository Writing 63

PART 4: Persuasive Writing 159

Credits and Permissions 188

Glossary 189

THEMATIC TABLE OF CONTENTS

1
The
Writing
Process

A writer's mind seems to be situated partly in the solar plexus, and partly in the head.

– Ethel Wilson

The writing process requires time to concentrate and organize, a comfortable familiarity with the topic, and ruthless editing for the final draft.

– Kathleen Darlington (student essayist)

INTRODUCTION

MOST WRITERS I KNOW, a group that includes students, teachers, professional writers, scribblers and jotters of all sorts, usually report that they experience the writing process as a varying combination of enjoyment and frustration. Sometimes the process of writing is fun. The words flow; the sentences create themselves in splendid order; the paragraphs follow one another as easily as clouds across a spring sky. Other times writing can be such a pain. You stare at the blank page; you stare out the window at the even blanker snow; you remember the unfinished bag of nachos on the counter downstairs (but you had better not indulge because this thing is due tomorrow). On most occasions, however, you simply write and rewrite, trying to find through hard work the language to express what you want to say. What all writers want to discover is a way to make this process as efficient as possible. You have a writing task or assignment. There is a deadline. You want to find a way to produce the best essay you can within the limits you have. Although there are no magical formulas for discovering this language, no single method that will solve all writing problems and fulfil all writing assignments, the writers I have known and read generally agree that there are certain things we can all do to make the writing process more efficient and effective. Each individual writer approaches each particular piece of writing in his or her own way; nonetheless, to be efficient and effective, writers must plan for and complete each stage of the writing process. Writing is a process, a series of stages, and writing that brings more enjoyment than frustration, as well as more success, will take each stage fully into account.

The essay writing process usually has five distinct but overlapping stages. You should begin to incorporate each stage into your writing process. In the rest of Part 1, you will find out more about each stage and how to apply it to your writing.

1. *Planning.* Successful writing requires sufficient time to think and write. You should develop a realistic writing schedule to ensure that you can produce high quality work by deadline.

2. *Prewriting.* Use informal strategies, such as free-writing and brainstorming, to develop a thesis, theme, or topic. Follow up with external research.

3. *Finding a focus.* You should have a clear idea of your purpose in writing the essay and of the intended audience for your essay.

4. *Organizing your ideas and writing a rough draft.* You need a solid framework on which to build an essay. Take time to organize your thoughts into a clearly ordered outline. Then — write!

5. *Reworking the essay.* Revision, editing, and proofreading are essential steps to an effective essay.

The writing process is recursive — that is, you may move back and forth freely during the process, from prewriting to research to revision to prewriting. For example, revision of your essay may lead you to reconsider your original thesis or main point. If so, you may need to do more prewriting and research to improve the focus of your essay.

PLANNING

THE NEXT FEW SECTIONS offer suggestions for planning, writing, and polishing your essays. This information will not benefit you, however, if your schedule forces you to pull together a few notes and hand in a first draft composed in the wee hours of the day the essay is due. Researching your topic and your audience, finding a purpose and focus, writing one or more drafts, and, finally, producing an attractive, error-free final copy all take time. To ensure that no step of the process receives less than adequate attention, you will need a writing schedule. First, list all the tasks that you have to do and the approximate time that you need to complete them. Adding up the days involved, you may discover that they extend well beyond your due date. In addition, you may have other assignments and work commitments. Your tasks, therefore, will have to overlap. The chart on the next page shows how you can schedule tasks to complete a major essay in two weeks. The overlap reflects not only your time limitations but also the recursive nature of the writing process.

PREWRITING

JUST AS BUILDERS must survey a site and gather building materials before construction can start, writers must gather information and ideas before they begin to compose. This process of searching can be divided into an internal search and an external search.

The Internal Search

The internal search is a process of discovering what you know about your subject and how that knowledge can help you plan and write your essay.

Work Schedule

Tasks	Days
	1 2 3 4 5 6 7 8 9 10 11 12 13 14 15
Conduct internal search	XXX
Plan external search	XXX
Analyze audience	XXX
Write outline	XXXXXXXX
Write first draft	XXXXXXXXXX X XX
Conduct external search	XXXXXXXXXXXXXXXX X XX
Revise	XXXXX X XX XX X
Edit	X XX XX X
Keyboard	X XX XX X
Proofread	X X
Prepare final copy	X X
Hand in	X

Several techniques exist for discovering this knowledge in a systematic and creative way.

Brainstorming

One familiar technique is brainstorming. You begin with a focus word and then free associate, writing down everything — every other word, phrase, or bit of information — that comes to mind when you think about the word. The idea is to recall everything you know about that word or concept. Do not try at first to organize your associations consciously. The following is a limited example.

Ecology (key word)

- the whole
- tree huggers
- interdependent
- harmony
- biosystems
- save the whales
- nuke the whales
- capitalists versus
- jobs versus
- the now

Once you have assembled your list, you can begin to try to see patterns in it, things that are similar or oppositions that recur. In this list, for example, we can see two patterns developing, one that repeats different ideas of the "whole" and one that first mocks and then counters with the "now." Later, you can use these kinds of patterns to begin to focus, organize, and structure your essay. In this example, the essay might develop around the opposition between the ecological concept of the "whole" and the economic necessities of "now." Another list would produce other patterns.

Brainstorming can also be used as a group activity to tap into new ideas. While you or the group are brainstorming, all ideas should be recorded, even if they seem redundant or off topic. Brainstorming should be a kind of intellectual play where you can spontaneously create and recreate whatever shapes come to mind.

Looping

Looping is a good method for finding a thesis statement. To loop, write continuously on a general topic for six to eight minutes, without revising or editing. Then read the results and summarize the controlling idea in one sentence. Continue to free-write, using the summary sentence as your starting point, for another six to eight minutes. Continue this process until you have developed a focussed thesis statement. For example, if you wrote for six minutes on the subject of humour, and your summary was that "laughter both divides and unites people," this statement would be the starting point for your next six minutes of free-writing. At the end of this free-writing session, you would write another summary sentence. You would continue this process until you could translate a summary sentence into a thesis statement.

Writing Idea Log

If you have ever had a great idea for an essay only to discover, when you sat down to write, that the idea had somehow disappeared, you will understand the usefulness of a writing idea log. In this log, you can freewrite, brainstorm, and draw. You can insert interesting visuals and collect stimulating articles from newspapers and magazines. Brief quotations from novels, poems, or discussions could be included. Writers have always used idea logs as a way of remembering writing ideas and playing with language in an expressive, informal way.

Visualization

This method is used to help people relax and overcome inhibitions. Allow your mind to journey back to a pleasant scene from your past: maybe a scene from childhood or a place you loved. Try to recapture the scene through brainstorming, recalling as much detail about it as you can. As you focus on specific details, jot down words and phrases that capture your experience. This technique can provide you with a rich source of images to add vividness and immediacy to personal, descriptive, and narrative essays.

Reading

One of the ways of discovering what you know about a subject and how you can shape that knowledge into an essay is by responding to how others have done that. In Margaret Laurence's "The Shack," for example, in the narrative section of this volume, she writes about one of her most loved places. Reading how she uses words to make us visualize her shack by the river can allow you both to visualize your own scene and to see how you can shape your own essay. You can respond by reshaping your memory of place into your specific form. We write essays, in fact, only because there are other essays, and our essays are written in response to them.

The External Search

After you have completed the first stages of your internal search, you may want to follow up your ideas by investigating other people's knowledge. The external search can include both what other people have written on the subject and what you can learn by talking to other people. The library is the obvious source of relevant written materials; some libraries also offer videotapes, films, recordings, and photographs. Through interviews, you can acquire information that has never been published.

Books

The best source of information about relevant books is the library cat-alogue. Most libraries use a microfiche catalogue (often called the COM catalogue), or a computerized system that lists all the books in the library by author, title, and subject. The subject headings are the ones the library uses to organize its book collection, and they may not match the terminol-ogy you are using. The library will have a guide to its subject headings in the reference section. Always check the guide before you use the subject cata-logue. If the holdings of the library you are using are not adequate for your research, a librarian can show you how to locate books from other libraries.

If you need specific facts and figures, your quickest source may be a reference book, such as an atlas, almanac, dictionary, or encyclopedia. These are usually kept together in a special section of the library. A librar-ian can help you find the most appropriate book for your purpose.

When extracting information, always keep notes on your sources, because you will need to acknowledge and document them in your essay. (See page 16.)

Periodicals

Periodicals (magazines and journals) contain information that is more up to date and often more specialized than that in books. Libraries generally keep current periodicals on the shelf, while back issues are bound into books. Back issues of newspapers are usually microfilmed. You can get access to all this material with a periodical index. These indexes appear regularly in book form; some cover popular Canadian and American magazines; some index articles on a particular subject, such as business; some cover only newspapers. Once you have located the name and date of the periodical you want, a librarian will help you locate it in the library or elsewhere.

On-Line Search

If your library subscribes to one or more databases, you can get a computer to search for the titles of relevant books and articles. Some will provide you with an abstract (brief summary) of an item or even a copy of an entire article. If you make your topic very specific, the computer can save you hours of time in cross-referencing. Many specialized databases are now available. A librarian can help you decide if a computer search would be cost-effective for your project.

The Interview

The interview can be an informative and revealing way to find our more about your subject. An effective interview requires good listening skills. Always remember that the focus of the interview is on the interviewee and that your role is to make the interviewee comfortable and willing to talk. Allow the interviewee to complete the answer to one question before you go on to your next question. Don't worry about pauses or breaks in the answer. Allow time for reflection. If you listen actively and carefully, you might hear a revealing comment that you want to follow up. If you find it difficult to follow an interview and record it on paper at the same time, use a tape recorder so that you can be free to listen attentively. (Make sure that you first get your interviewee's permission.)

An effective interviewer is an effective researcher. Research helps generate good questions that will, in turn, generate good answers. For example, if you were interviewing a Member of Parliament about a controversial government policy, you would be wise to search for current information in newspapers, periodicals, and government documents before going to the interview. Intelligent and accurate questions show that you value the time the interviewee is graciously giving you.

An interview has several advantages as a researching technique:

1. You can secure first-hand information on a topic instead of relying totally on secondary sources.

2. The information in your essay will more closely reflect your voice, since you design the questions for the interview.

3. The interview may take your search in another direction, reflecting the recursive nature of the writing process.

4. You will hone your listening skills. This training will assist you in all aspects of your writing.

FINDING A FOCUS

I F YOU HAVE PERSISTED in your internal and external search, you will now have a provisional thesis, or main theme, and a collection of notes and ideas that can be used to expand and develop your theme. However, before you can transform this diverse assortment of thoughts and inspirations into an effective essay, you need to decide what you want to do with them. You need to find a focus.

Establishing the Purpose

You can begin to find a focus by asking yourself a basic question: Why am I writing this essay? What is my purpose? Do you want to express something, some experience, emotion, or memory that is important to you? Do you want to explain how something works? Do you want to influence the attitude or behaviour of other people? These three questions correspond to the three main types of writing contained in this book: expressive, expository, and persuasive. You can begin to find a focus by considering what type of writing is most appropriate to your purpose.

You can then explore and develop your purpose by asking yourself more specific questions. What do you really want to express? Why do you want to explain how this particular thing works? To what idea, position, or behaviour do you want to move your audience? In order to find a focus, you must be certain what you want to do with the essay. Given the recursive nature of the writing process, however, you can discover your actual purpose at any stage. The important thing is to keep your purpose always in mind.

Considering Your Audience

How you go about achieving the purpose of your essay will depend largely on the nature of your audience. Anyone in the performing arts (actor, musician, singer, comedian) takes into consideration the backgrounds, interests, and ages of the audience when choosing an approach to a particular performance. Similarly, a writer must study the audience to know what language techniques will be suitable and effective. You will have to consider choice of vocabulary, level of difficulty, tone, and need for background information, among other elements.

For example, what would you need to take into consideration about your audience if you were asked to write two essays, one directed to the Minister of Health and the other for your student newspaper, arguing for the implementation of a smoke-free environment at your college? Because the Minister of Health is presumably well informed on the intricacies of your subject, your essay, in order to be persuasive, would need to include thorough research on the subject. You would draw on statistics, studies, and government reports to convince the minister that your argument is valid. At the same time, because of the minister's broad knowledge, you might not have to spend as much time giving background information. Conversely, in your essay to your fellow students, you would need to provide background information on the hazards of smoking and second-hand smoke. You could use a less formal tone, since your essay is meant to be an article in a newspaper. Audience awareness, then, means speaking or writing in terms the audience will relate to and understand.

Limiting Your Subject

One of the most frequent weaknesses in essays is a lack of focus because the student has failed to limit the subject of the essay. Instructors often give students very general essay topics on very large subjects like "English–French Relations in Canada" or "Aboriginal Self-Government." Such subjects are much too broad and complex to be covered adequately in an essay of 1500 or 2000 words. If you do not limit your essay to one aspect of such a large subject (for example, the situation of francophones living outside Quebec), your essay will be superficial, probably disorganized, and full of vague generalizations and unsupported opinions. If you limit your topic, you will be able to offer a unified, focussed treatment, with supporting evidence for all of the points that you make.

Writing the Thesis Statement

A focussed essay will present a point of view, take a position, or offer a line of argument throughout the essay. The entire focus of the essay, however, will most often be presented in a single sentence, the thesis statement. The thesis statement articulates the central point or points of the essay. In expressive essays, the thesis may often be implicit or expressed in a controlling point of view, rather than in one sentence. In expository or persuasive essays, the thesis statement is usually placed within the first paragraph, generally as the last sentence.

The thesis statement is the essay in miniature. The order of the points in the sentence should usually reflect the order of the points in the essay. In other words, the thesis statement should be predictive of the essay to follow. The statement will create certain expectations in the reader that the essay will fulfil. The thesis statement should not simply repeat the assignment or state the obvious. The statement should articulate the focus of the essay completely and clearly. The thesis statement should also not just be a summary of the essay; rather, the statement should develop a point of view, position, or argument.

Although you should begin focussing on a thesis statement from the earliest stages of the writing process, the actual sentence you use might be the last one you write. As you discover and develop your purpose, your focus will change, and the thesis statement will necessarily change with it. Above all, try to be flexible: rewrite the thesis statement as many times as you find necessary.

Ideally, the thesis should offer a point of view or position (in an expressive or expository essay) or a line of argument (in a persuasive essay). This statement should work as a linchpin, controlling the organization of your ideas and the presentation of information through the course of your essay. To see how closely the whole essay revolves around the thesis statement, look at the organizational outline of "Violence in the Media" below.

Discovering Your Rhetorical Mode

As another way of finding a focus, you will have to decide or discover what rhetorical mode will be most appropriate to your purpose. A mode is a particular form of writing, and this book is divided into ten basic modes. These modes overlap — narrative necessarily includes descriptive and vice versa; classification often includes definition and vice versa — but one mode will be more appropriate for your purpose than the others and finding a focus will entail the selection and development of a mode. In her essay "Violence in the Media," for example, Karen Kowalski was concerned to find the similarities and differences between the treatment of a certain theme in two movies. Obviously, her rhetorical mode would be comparison and contrast. This mode has certain structural or organizational possibilities in it that Karen used to discover and develop her essay. Each mode contains within it certain possibilities that can be developed in various ways. Finding a focus and moving to the next stage of the writing process often depends upon discovering the way in which a mode can be developed into an essay.

ORGANIZING YOUR IDEAS AND WRITING A ROUGH DRAFT

O NCE YOU HAVE FOUND YOUR FOCUS, you have laid the foundation for your essay and can proceed to more detailed planning.

Drafting an Outline

An essay could be defined as a sequence of words, sentences, and paragraphs presented in a certain order or structure. A crucial stage of the writing process is the discovery of this order or structure. There is no single formula for this order. The order should develop out of your purpose, thesis, and rhetorical mode. Karen Kowalski's mode was comparison and contrast. In this mode, you usually work with two entities, isolating and analyzing various features of both. This mode allows for certain structural possibilities, as you compare and contrast, say, three features of the first entity with the second. These structural possibilities can eventually form a very precise kind of symmetry. To illustrate how Karen has taken advantage of these possibilities, we have provided an organizational analysis of her essay. This analysis, we should note, is not a working outline, but a map of the finished essay depicted as an outline. Obviously, in the process of writing Karen moved by stages to this final form with its neat symmetries.

This outline begins with the thesis statement. Each paragraph is then headed by a topic sentence. A topic sentence functions for the paragraph as the thesis statement does for the entire essay.

Outline of "Violence in the Media"

Thesis Statement   Although the violence of both *Dead Ringers* and *Road Warrior* is disturbing, the representation of violence in *Dead Ringers* as implicit, realistic, and psychological is more harmful in its effects than the representation of violence in *Road Warrior*.

Paragraph 3

Topic Sentence   The way in which the violence differs in two movies becomes evident when contrasting the portrayal of violence against women.

Evidence   1. Violence against women in *Dead Ringers* is continuous throughout the movie and is implied; the focus is on the sounds and facial expressions of the gynecological patients, which gives the audience more opportunity to exercise their imaginations.

2. Violence against women in *Road Warrior* is in one scene only and is explicit; the scene leaves nothing to the imagination.

3. Imagination plays a key role in the effects of violence; violence is more effective when the audience exercise their imaginations.

Paragraph 4

Topic Sentence   Another way to explain why the violence in *Dead Ringers* has more of an impact than the violence in *Road Warrior* is to contrast the situations of both movies.

Evidence   1. Situation of *Dead Ringers* is realistic; events occur in the present and revolve around a real part of our lives — the doctor's office.

2. Situation of *Road Warrior* is futuristic and fantastic; the setting is unfamiliar and audience can't relate to it.

3. Audience can relate better to a realistic setting than a fantastic one, so *Dead Ringers* has more impact.

Paragraph 5

Topic Sentence   A third and final way to explain why the violence in *Dead Ringers* has more impact on an audience than the violence in *Road Warrior* is to contrast the psychological and physical aspects of the movies.

Evidence   1. Violence in *Dead Ringers* is psychological; it results from the dementia of the characters, and their psychological difficulties tie the audience to the movie.

2. Violence in *Road Warrior* is purely physical; purely "rack 'em and hack 'em" movie.

> 3. Audience is more affected by psychological violence because they have a greater ability to identify with it than with physical violence.

Conclusion   When the members of an audience are given the opportunity to exercise their imaginations and to experience violence in a realistic setting they can relate to, the violence in the movie will have a greater impact on them.

When drafting the outline for your essay, you may find it helpful merely to jot down a few words on a scrap of paper. Most students, however, find a well organized outline, using either complete sentences (as in our example) or point form, the most effective way to organize their material before writing their first draft. Moreover, the outline will give you an opportunity to ensure that all of your topic sentences relate back to your thesis and that all of the material in each paragraph is connected to the topic sentence that introduces it.

As you begin to organize your notes into an outline, remember what you have established about your purpose, audience, and rhetorical mode. If your essay is essentially descriptive, you will probably want to begin with the familiar and lead into the new and the unfamiliar. If you are persuading, you will have to decide whether to state your thesis at the beginning and then expand it with explanation or examples, or to present your evidence first and then lead into your thesis. After you have arranged your material into a tentative outline, test it for the following elements:

Clarity

Is the direction of your essay evident from the opening sentence? Does each topic sentence clearly relate to your thesis statement? Is the information in your paragraphs clearly connected to the topic sentences that begin them? Can the reader clearly see how the evidence in each paragraph relates to the essay's main point?

Coherence

Is your essay logical? Are your conclusions or arguments supported by evidence that is sufficient and relevant? Have you made logical connections between the parts of your essay?

Unity

Is there any material that seems out of place or unrelated to the main idea? Is there information included that does not contribute to the main point of your essay or that may even contradict it? Does the point of view seem consistent?

Your first outline may have to be considerably modified once you begin to write, as you will learn in the next section. Nevertheless, the initial outlining process forces you to read your notes selectively, think about the relationships among your ideas, and write with clarity, coherence, and unity in mind.

Writing the First Draft

Writing a first draft is a demanding task. Even the most complete outline will leave a huge gap to be filled; words and phrases must be transformed into whole sentences that are concise, clear, unified, smoothly connected, and mechanically correct. If you try to achieve perfect results in every area of your essay as you go along, you will inevitably succumb to writer's block as you lose sight of the purpose and focus of your essay. The key to writing a first draft is to keep writing. Don't stop.

REWORKING THE ESSAY

O NCE YOU HAVE COMPLETED THE FIRST DRAFT, you need to evaluate the results of your efforts. Some writers like to put their first draft in a drawer and let it sit there for a few days. They will then take it out of the drawer and read it again. This rereading and rethinking of the first draft usually leads to substantive revision.

Substantive Revision

Substantive revision is more than merely editing or proofreading. As the words imply, it means re-viewing or re-seeing the substance of your work. This process can involve making major changes in the organization of the whole essay. For example, your thesis may need to be significantly altered if you find that your first draft does not support your original argument or point of view. Or you may decide to change the organization of your essay, necessitating changes in the content and order of your paragraphs. The process of writing and revising is akin to the glass blowing process. Glass blowers work toward achieving well balanced shapes that are both functional and attractive. If their efforts produce flaws or weaknesses in structure, they return the glass to the furnace to begin the process over again. Eventually, the glass meets their specifications. Likewise, when you re-see your essay and discover that it does not meet your specifications, in terms of the purpose you are trying to achieve and the audience you are attempting to reach, you should continue revising it until it does.

Checklist for Substantive Revision

Organization

1. Is your thesis clearly stated?
2. Does the opening paragraph orient the reader to the essay to follow?
3. Do your supporting arguments follow logically?
4. Does each paragraph contribute to the development of your thesis?
5. Are your paragraphs in a logical sequence?
6. Is there a smooth and logical transition from one sentence to another and from one paragraph to the next?

Content

1. Does the content reflect the results of your internal and external search?
2. Do you have enough supporting details?
3. Are the supporting details relevant and accurate?
4. Will the supporting details be understood by your intended audience?

Editing

If your substantive revision has produced a structure that embodies your ideas in a clear, convincing way, you are ready to move on to the next step: editing. Editing is the process of fine-tuning word choice and sentence structure and eliminating errors in grammar, spelling, and punctuation. To ensure that you have chosen words that convey your ideas accurately, read your essay all the way through, marking any words that strike you as dubious or inexact. At the same time, underline any words or phrases that seem to be overused. Do not stop to fix anything until you have finished reading.

If you aren't sure of the exact meaning of any words, check them in a dictionary. Try to use a large unabridged dictionary because it will illustrate the correct uses of a word and it will distinguish subtle differences. If a word is repeated with distracting frequency, look for a synonym in a dictionary or thesaurus. Check the definition of any synonym from the thesaurus in the dictionary to ensure that the synonym applies to your context.

After making any changes, read your essay again. Is your sentence length varied? Overuse of short sentences makes your writing seem abrupt and unsophisticated, while too many long sentences strain the reader's powers of concentration and increase the likelihood of grammar or punctuation errors. Make changes that will help your essay flow more smoothly.

Check to make sure that you have acknowledged any quotations or second-hand information and that your references are complete and consistent in style. If you have quoted from a book or an article or borrowed ideas from another writer, you must document your sources. This documentation enables your reader to check on your source and gather further information and is a mark of intellectual honesty. You will document the author's name, the title of the work and of the book or periodical it appears in, the place of publication, name of publisher and date of publication (for a book), the volume number and date of publication (for a periodical), and the page numbers of the material you are citing.

Both as a matter of style and to avoid confusion, you need to follow a consistent, accepted style of listing all these data. There are several systems of documentation now in use. You may have used endnotes and a bibliography in preparing an essay. The system of author/date citation is now more broadly accepted. Find out whether your instructor prefers a particular style of documentation. If you have a choice, the MLA (Modern Language Association) style is appropriate for essays in the humanities, while for social sciences the APA (American Psychological Association) style is favoured. Most libraries have books and style sheets illustrating the various documentation systems.

Finally, check the spelling and other mechanics of your essay. Don't let surface errors detract from its effect.

Checklist for Editing

Word Choice

1. Is the language level suitable for the intended audience?

2. Have you defined any technical terms that your audience may not know?

3. Have you verified the meaning of any words of which you were unsure?

4. Is your vocabulary specific and interesting?

5. Have you replaced overworked words and phrases with synonyms?

6. Does your word choice reflect the intended tone of your essay?

Sentence Structure

1. Have you used a variety of sentence structures?

2. Have you cut down sentences that were too long, complex, or difficult to understand?

3. Have you used short sentences appropriately for emphasis?

4. Have you eliminated sentence fragments and run-on sentences?

5. Are all the sentences smoothly linked?

6. Can each sentence be easily read aloud?

Paragraphs

1. Are the paragraphs too long or too short?

2. Is each paragraph a single idea fully developed?

3. Does each paragraph have a topic sentence?

4. Does each paragraph connect with the one before and the one after?

5. Do the introductory and concluding paragraphs do all the things that first and last paragraphs should in order to begin and end an essay successfully?

Mechanics

1. Have you observed standard punctuation rules?

2. Have you checked the spelling of any word of which you were unsure?

3. Have you double-checked for any grammar errors that you commit frequently?

4. If you have used outside sources, are they documented according to a consistent convention?

Proofreading

To ensure that you have a professional and finely finished product, proof-read your edited draft (or have it proofread) to catch any errors in keyboarding, as well as any other errors missed in revising and editing. A computer will make it easier for you to produce a clean, error-free copy.

Finally, look at the physical appearance of your essay. Make sure it looks neat and professional — double-spaced in a clear typeface (whether produced by a typewriter or computer), with generous margins.

After you have devoted the necessary time and attention to all of these steps, you can sit back, relax, and feel confident about a job well done: your essay is complete!

2
Expressive
Writing

I put a piece of paper under my
pillow, and when I could not sleep
I wrote in the dark.

– Henry David Thoreau

The constant challenge is to
reproduce the mental experience
in an interpretable written form.

– Catherine Figura
(student essayist)

INTRODUCTION

W HAT IS AN ESSAY? An essay is simply any short, nonfiction, prose composition. This definition allows a vast scope. The essay comes in many forms and fulfils many functions. In this book we consider three main types of writing: expressive, expository, and persuasive. Most essays will fit into one of these broad categories, although some will fall in between. For example, we discuss "My Private Collection of Memories," by Catherine Figura, as a classification essay — a mode of expository writing — but it certainly contains elements of expressive writing. Within these categories, we examine several rhetorical modes (styles or approaches to writing). In reality, many essays will include elements of more than one mode; almost all essays contain some description and some examples.

Expressive writing, which is also known as "personal writing," encompasses all writing of a personal, highly subjective nature. The shortest and most common form is the diary or journal, in which the author simply records the day's events or emotions. Greatly expanded, the diary becomes an autobiography. This form of prose has many purposes: to narrate, to describe, to amuse, to explain. Often elements of all these rhetorical modes are combined. In any case, the topic is of personal significance to the writer, and the greatest challenge is to evoke reciprocal interest in the reader. In the samples that follow, you will encounter essays that reflect the personalities of the writers. All of the writers expose their sensibilities, sometimes their sense of humour, and sometimes their deepest emotions. The final goal of expressive writing is to sensitize, entertain, comfort, or move the reader. For the writer, the benefits are even greater. The writing process not only satisfies an innate need to write; it can also help the writer solve a problem or at least come to terms with a difficult aspect of life.

THE DESCRIPTIVE ESSAY

A DESCRIPTIVE ESSAY is an extended piece of writing that primarily uses descriptive language — language that paints a picture or details the characteristics of someone, something, or someplace — for a particular purpose. The authors in this section use description for the following purposes:

- To evoke the culture and values that shape an East Indian woman's world, by describing a day in her life (in "A Touch from the East," by Daggy Brunst).

- To share the sensory experience of skiing, from putting on the clothes and equipment to enjoying the beauty of the mountains (in "The Skier," by Nancy Dorey).

- To describe and evoke the place most loved and deeply remembered (in "The Shack," by Margaret Laurence).

- To show the richness of life that we often miss passing just outside our window (in "The View from the Businessman's Corner Window," by Robert Newman).

Techniques of Description

Observation and Measurement

To form a mental image of an object or process, your reader needs some objective details that convey the appearance, texture, volume, or other quality of the thing described. For example, the word "book" conveys little to a reader. However, the phrase "a small book the size of the palm of your hand, bound in smooth, red leather" gives the reader a vivid picture of the book about which you are talking. Certain kinds of description, such as instructions, procedures, specifications, and accident reports, require very specific, accurate details. In some cases, exact measurements may be required. Nothing should be omitted. The writer who is seeking merely to entertain, however, can be both more selective and more general. In any case, close observation of important detail remains the foundation of a good descriptive essay.

Comparison

Often a reader can grasp something unfamiliar more quickly if the writer describes it by comparing it to something familiar. The storage and retrieval system of the human brain might be better understood when compared to a computer. The taste of spices like fennel and anise could be compared to that of licorice, or the colour of a dress could be compared to that of a robin's egg or a poppy.

Figurative Language

A writer uses figurative language to convey not only objective information about the size, colour, or sound of a thing, but also the writer's subjective impression of it. Consider the last sentence from "The View from the Businessman's Corner Window": "The water cooler's smooth symmetry is broken only by fleeting reflections of life's sweet breath tickling the panes of glass in the businessman's corner office window." The reader is left with much more than a visual image.

To describe an object or experience using figurative language means to compare it to something that does not look or sound or smell the same, but instead conveys the same feeling. This implied comparison is called a *simile* if you use *like* or *as* — "His voice was like wind in winter trees." If the comparison does not use *like* or *as*, it is called a *metaphor*. For example, a person who overcame his drug addiction described the experience using metaphor in the following way: "Breaking the drug habit reminded me of the struggle the East Germans had in breaking down the Wall. When that wall was opened, they had access to the opportunities beyond the Wall. I had to break down my wall of drug dependency to see new opportunities for my life."

Using any of the above techniques of description can add resonance to your essay and can effectively engage your reader in the experience you are describing.

Daggy Brunst

Born of Russian and German parents, Daggy began her schooling in Montreal and graduated from Middlebury College, Vermont, with a BA in Education and French. "Then for thirteen years I roamed the East, flitting from the exotic to the ascetic, steeping myself in culture, reading scriptures, and teaching English. I returned to Canada in July of 1988 with my husband." Now Daggy has completed her TESL certificate and is in the Master's program for Applied Linguistics at Concordia University.

She explains that the hardest part of writing this story was "telling the truth as I had seen and experienced it, unclouded by Western eyes. My aim was not to convince, but to show and let the reader decide."

A Touch from the East

S
ARADA LAY ON THE STRAW MAT, awake but reluctant to rise. She *1*
sniffed the aroma of fresh coffee carried by the breeze and felt her
body warm and relaxed, secure with her husband's protective hand
resting gently on her breast. She nudged her head into the hollow of his
shoulder and dozed, until the high-pitched squabble of tired women trying
to fill their pots of water from a single trickling tap on the street broke
into her intimacy.

In the dark of the tiny backyard, unobserved, she removed her crumpled *2*
sari, pulled her long black hair into a knot, and took her bath; dipping the
brass pitcher into a wooden tub, she poured the cold water over her head
and shivered. Instead of soap, she used a piece of turmeric root, rubbed
into a paste on a rock. After she had smeared it on her body and rinsed it
off, her skin still glowed with the yellow dye. On top of her white petti-
coat and bodice, she wore a crisp, starched sari. Her oiled hair glistened and,
like her mother and grandmother—in fact, like every woman in the land—
she wore it neatly parted in the middle and hanging in a single thick braid
down her back. Only if she became a widow would her hair hang loose,
uncombed and neglected until the barber shaved it off.

Before the dawn broke, household duties awaited her. With a broom *3*
of dried grass she swept the house. Outside, on the hard earth surface, she
scattered water mixed with dung, swept smooth the holes ants had made,

and then, with rice flour pinched between thumb and index finger, she drew an intricate design of lines on the damp surface. Only once, when her father died, had she not drawn this lucky symbol to protect the house. Above the entrance, clinging to a bamboo frame, grew a thick root of jasmine. She picked the sweet-smelling flowers, along with some red hibiscus. Inside, the vegetables were boiling. She stirred them, and entered the pooja room. An oil lamp cast flickering light upon the dream-like faces of the gods. Some smiled in benign repose; others, their mouths agape, tongues protruding, lusted to devour evil. Inhabiting the shelf facing east stood Parvati, Mother of the Universe, moulded in bronze. Beside her sat her pot-bellied Son, sporting an elephant's head. Sarada reverently decorated Mother and Son with jasmine, the other gods with red hibiscus. In front of every nose she wafted a burning incense stick. To rouse them from their night of rest, she sang an epic of their glory, and, as the song rose from her heart, she felt a yearning for their touch. Then she knelt, placed her head on the floor, and begged the gods to keep her husband safe.

4   Mama called from a corner in the kitchen where she crouched hump-backed, her shaven head covered by the end of an ochre sari. Her pendulous earlobes hung empty. Since Papa's cremation she had, as is the custom, removed all her golden ornaments—for what use is a woman's beauty if her husband is dead? She sat clutching the cup of hot milk Sarada gave her, sipping it slowly, trying to fill her wrinkled frame with nourishment before the week's pilgrimage, which would try to assure a peaceful rest to Papa's soul.

5   The rice had finished cooking. Soon the smell of heating oil and sizzling chilies tickled Sarada's nose. She packed her husband's lunch into seven containers: three different vegetables, curd, rice, a sweet, and a pickle. Then she started breakfast, grinding up coconut chutney to accompany the fermented batter steaming into rice cakes. It was now seven o'clock; time to wake him. When touched, he yawned and turned over, so she massaged his back. As quickly as she could, she filled the tub with hot water, soaped and rinsed his body, rubbed him dry, then buttoned his shirt. After breakfast, with a kiss, he left for work. While the clothes were soaking, she made pickles, cutting lemons and mixing them with salt. The rice needed cleaning—it was filled with chaff and stones—and the coriander, too. Then she ground rice and lentils into a gurgling paste for the next day's cakes. After lunch she pounded rice with a heavy wooden pestle, sifted out the fine flour and made it into a dry dough, which she rolled into paper-thin disks and put in the sun to dry. Fried in oil, they would make a nice snack for Ravi when he came home from work.

6   Even before he knocked, she heard his footsteps outside and went to greet him. A look of pity crossed her face as she relieved him of a heavy

bag of vegetables, for it was her duty to carry. He was a good man, and didn't like his wife to go out.

   She hung up his work clothes; he sat on the mat she spread for him. As 7 usual, he drank his tea and munched a snack while reading the newspaper. To please her, he had bought their favourite vegetable, a tiny type of spinach, so Sarada began the tedious task of cleaning it. Two hours passed before she steamed and churned it, cooked fresh rice, and made a pepper soup. Then she worshipped the gods, offering them a tiny plate of food. By now she was hungry and she called her husband for supper. He sat cross-legged on the floor in front of a huge banana leaf plate, piled high with a mound of steaming rice. Just as she was about to serve herself, an unexpected guest arrived. Immediately she stood up and receded respectfully, with folded palms in front of her downcast eyes. Ravi courteously invited the guest for dinner. The pungent taste increased the men's appetites; Sarada served them until they belched loudly. While they chatted she washed the greasy cooking pots. Later, for a few minutes she stood behind her spouse listening to their conversation, till he turned, and asked her to make tea. Long after their guest had left, and husband and wife were in bed, Sarada put her hand on his chest and tried to fall asleep to the sound of his soothing snoring, but the empty feeling in the pit of her stomach kept her awake.

READING

1. What is the significance of Brunst's title? Do you think it is an effective title? Why or why not?

2. Even though this is primarily descriptive writing, chronology is used. How much time is covered and how is its passage indicated?

3. A successful essay is coherent: sentences flow smoothly because the author has made good use of transitions. Look at paragraph five and select the transitional words the author has used.

4. Varying sentence type and sentence length is another way to ensure paragraphs flow smoothly. Study the sentences in paragraph three and indicate whether they are similar or varied.

5. A good essayist or short-story writer gives readers the background they need to understand the characters without awkwardly disrupting the narrative flow. Study paragraphs two and four closely. What do these paragraphs tell us about Sarada and her mother, other than what they are doing at that particular moment? What do they tell us about the society in which they live? Does the essay impart this information smoothly?

6. How does Brunst emphasize that Sarada's life is bound by ritual and tradition?

7. How would you describe the role of the husband in this household?

8. What is revealed about the nature of Sarada's domestic role in the final sentence of the essay? Is this an effective conclusion? Why or why not?

9. Study the introduction and conclusion. Do the beginning and ending give the essay unity?

FROM READING TO WRITING

1. Record in your notebook a typical day in your life. Think about your role as a woman or a man in society and your attitude toward that role. Put down your thoughts and feelings in your notebook. Then write a narrative essay about one day in your life, using description to tell the reader about your role in society and your feelings about that role.

2. Interview someone who grew up in Canada more than fifty years ago and ask that person to take you through a typical day in his or her early life. Pay particular attention to detail. Ask what life was like before the days of cars, television, refrigerators. Write a vivid description of a typical day in an earlier era.

Nancy Dorey

*Once she starts writing, Nancy has difficulty stopping. However,
she also finds that it takes her about four drafts before the work
begins to sound right. "I have always had a pen in my hand, either to
write or draw," she explains. Nancy is a student in the Fine Arts
program at Concordia University.*

The Skier

U NDER THE FETAL WARMTH of a heavy quilt, muscles stretch and   1
groan, sore from yesterday's turns and spills. The room is dark;
outside it's snowing. Sweaty ski clothes are waiting to be put on
again. An early morning breakfast is eaten in haste. Stiff boots must once
again encase sore feet before you can venture out into the astounding
silence of falling snow. You wade through it, shin deep, boots crunching,
skis on shoulder; the whole world is white.

The lift is silent and snow covered. You are early. And so, with cold   2
feet and impatience, you share the falling snow with a few others, all waiting while stomping their feet to keep warm.

The lift operator arrives and is soon sweeping snow off the lift with an   3
overworked broom. White fluff scatters in clouds to reveal dark, greasy
metal. A cough, a hum, gears clank, and the chairs lurch into motion,
beginning their daily, repetitive journey. The operator nods and you slide
into place; the chair comes and you glide upward into the still descending
snow.

The silent spruce are black against the sombre sky. Suddenly, there's a   4
hint of blue and the falling snow is thinner now. You watch as a single
crystal fairy dances down from the sky; another taps you on the nose.

The sky is blue now, the distant peaks etched silver against it. Three   5
more towers and you are in the sun. The ramp arrives and your skis cut
through the ridges as you slide off the chair, down into two feet of
sparkling virgin snow. You struggle through the drift, then begin working
your skis through the wind-packed snow toward the mountain's lip.
Looking down, you see the quick, easy runs below, and above, the more
remote slopes still lost in the tattered patch of a cloud that remains in the
lee of the mountain. You start creeping upward. The track is long gone;
you must guess a line and begin the long journey to the top.

6   Morning sweat, grunts, and four-letter words abound. The sky is a dazzling blue; the snow sparkles. You go slowly, picking up one ski at a time, stomping down a place for it, then shifting upward one step. Progress is slow, and in places it seems nonexistent.

7   Struggling still; the lower slopes are distant now; the top still hides. Sweat, sunglare, and aching muscles — what a way to start the day — but on you go, thrashing upward.

8   The top draws near — edging slowly, so slowly, closer. Sweat has collected around your waist; clothing half on, half off, goggles up one minute and down the next, eyes squinting into the glare and distance. The final few feet take forever: finally you collapse, panting, exhausted, in the snow.

9   On the ridge the wind is cutting and stray snow sandpapers your face. Beneath your feet the mountain drops away. Amid the silver minarets of the Canadian Rockies you whisper a chant and contemplate your first turn: that first soft sifting of snow, mind, and body. On the very edge you hesitate, lost in the mountains, snow, and sky. Finally goggles come down; bindings are checked. No words are spoken.

10   Softly you are away. You turn gently, slowly, then turn again. Turns, more turns, each one like a waltz. You watch the slow arc of arm and pole, feel the flex, turn, and twist of muscles and tendons as you come down the mountain. Your skis are free, arcing around and down into the snow again, creating a fine wave that washes up and over you.

11   One final steep pitch and you land in an explosion of snow. This time the snow is very deep and you are seconds emerging from it. The surface of the snow is fluid. Whiteness surrounds you again — where is up? Where is the mountaintop? Where is down? Where are you going? Will you survive?

12   Down and down, through the last few remaining turns to the bottom. The last turn, you carve it wide and slow, coming around to look back up the mountain.

13   Soon others arrive and walk across the flat ground and into the crowd. There in the middle of the mechanical madness of a bigtime ski resort you stop, skis on your shoulder, and lose yourself in the wonder of skiing.

READING

1. What do you consider to be the most powerful descriptive passages, phrases, or words in this essay? Why are they powerful?

2. Develop an outline that illustrates how Dorey has organized her essay.

3. Why does the author use the second person in the narration of her essay?

4. What is the thesis? Is it explicit or implied?

5. How many different ways does the essay describe the look and condition of the snow?

6. Good opening paragraphs establish the tone and setting for the whole essay. Are the introductory paragraphs effective?

7. Why does the author use the present tense in this essay? Is her use of the present tense effective? Why or why not?

FROM READING TO WRITING

1. Have you experienced an exhilarating moment (or moments) while playing a sport? Record these experiences in your notebook, jotting down as many details as you can remember. Select the most memorable experience. Then write a descriptive paragraph about it. (Your audience is someone who has never experienced the thrill of this sport.)

2. Watching a sport can sometimes be as exciting as participating. Recall a sporting event that made a deep impression on you, and write as much as you can remember about it in your notebook. From your notes, construct an outline for a narrative essay; then write the essay. Pay attention to your vocabulary, using descriptive language as much as possible. Try to develop a sense of suspense. (Your audience is someone who is as keen about the sport as you are, but who hasn't seen this event.)

Margaret Laurence

Margaret Laurence, born in Neepawa, Manitoba, in 1926, was one of Canada's most celebrated and important novelists. Her groundbreaking novels The Stone Angel *(1964) and* The Diviners *(1974) opened and explored new territory in the Canadian literary landscape. The following essay appeared in her volume* Heart of a Stranger *(1976). She died in Lakefield, Ontario, in 1987.*

The Shack

1   THE MOST LOVED PLACE, for me, in this country has in fact been many places. It has changed throughout the years, as I and my circumstances have changed. I haven't really lost any of the best places from the past, though. I may no longer inhabit them, but they inhabit me, portions of memory, presences in the mind. One such place was my family's summer cottage at Clear Lake in Riding Mountain National Park, Manitoba. It was known to us simply as The Lake. Before the government piers and the sturdy log staircases down to the shore were put in, we used to slither with an exhilarating sense of peril down the steep homemade branch and dirt shelf-steps, through the stands of thin tall spruce and birch trees slender and graceful as girls, passing moss-hairy fallen logs and the white promise of wild strawberry blossoms, until we reached the sand and the hard bright pebbles of the beach at the edge of the cold spring-fed lake where at nights the loons still cried eerily, before too much humanshriek made them move away north.

2   My best place at the moment is very different, although I guess it has some of the attributes of that long-ago place. It is a small cedar cabin on the Otonabee river in southern Ontario. I've lived three summers there, writing, bird-watching, river-watching. I sometimes feel sorry for the people in speedboats who spend their weekends zinging up and down the river at about a million miles an hour. For all they're able to see, the riverbanks might just as well be green concrete and the river itself flowing with molten plastic.

3   Before sunup, I'm wakened by birdvoices and, I may say, birdfeet clattering and thumping on the cabin roof. Cursing only slightly, I get up *temporarily*, for the pre-dawn ritual of lighting a small fire in the old black woodstove (mornings are chilly here, even in summer) and looking out at

the early river. The waters have a lovely spooky quality at this hour, entirely mist-covered, a secret meeting of river and sky.

By the time I get up to stay, the mist has vanished and the river is a 4 clear ale-brown, shining with sun. I drink my coffee and sit looking out to the opposite shore, where the giant maples are splendidly green now and will be trees of flame in the fall of the year. Oak and ash stand among the maples, and the grey skeletons of the dead elms, gauntly beautiful even in death. At the very edge of the river, the willows are everywhere, water-related trees, magic trees, pale green in early summer, silvergreen in late summer, greengold in autumn.

I begin work, and every time I lift my eyes from the page and glance out- 5 side, it is to see some marvel or other. The joyous dance-like flight of the swallows. The orange-black flash of the orioles who nest across the river. The amazing takeoff of a red-winged blackbird, revealing like a swiftly unfolded fan the hidden scarlet in those dark wings. The flittering of the goldfinches, who always travel in domestic pairs, he gorgeous in black-patterned yellow feathers, she (alas) drabber in greenish grey-yellow.

A pair of great blue herons have their huge unwieldy nest about half a 6 mile upriver, and although they are very shy, occasionally through the open door I hear a sudden approaching rush of air (yes, you can *hear* it) and look up quickly to see the magnificent unhurried sweep of those powerful wings. The only other birds which can move me so much are the Canada geese in their autumn migration flight, their far-off wilderness voices the harbinger of winter.

Many boats ply these waterways, and all of them are given mental 7 gradings of merit or lack of it, by me. Standing low in the estimation of all of us along this stretch of the river are some of the big yachts, whose ego-tripping skippers don't have the courtesy to slow down in cottage areas and whose violent wakes scour out our shorelines. Ranking highest in my good books are the silent unpolluting canoes and rowboats, and next to them, the small outboard motorboats put-putting along and carrying patient fishermen, and the homemade houseboats, unspeedy and some-how cosy-looking, decorated lovingly with painted birds or flowers or gaudy abstract splodges.

In the quiet of afternoon, if no boats are around, I look out and see 8 the half-moon leap of a fish, carp or muskie, so instantaneous that one has the impression of having seen not a fish but an arc of light.

The day moves on, and about four o'clock Linda and Susan from the 9 nearby farm arrive. I call them the Girls of the Pony Express. Accompanied by dogs and laughter, they ride their horses into my yard, kindly bringing my mail from the rural route postbox up the road. For several summers it was Old Jack who used to drive his battered Volkswagen up to fetch the mail. He was one of the best neighbours and most remarkable men I've ever known. As a boy of eighteen, he had homesteaded a hundred miles north of Regina. Later, he'd been a skilled toolmaker with Ford. He'd travelled to South America and done many amazing things. He was a man whose life had taught him a lot of wisdom. After his much-loved wife died, he moved out here to the river, spending as short a winter as possible in Peterborough, and getting back into his cottage the first of anyone in the spring, when the river was still in flood and he could only get in and out, hazardously, by boat. I used to go out in his boat with him, late afternoons, and we would dawdle along the river, looking at the forest stretches and the open rolling farmlands and vast old barns, and at the smaller things closeby, the heavy luxuriance of ferns at the water's rim, the dozens of snapping turtles with unblinking eyes, all sizes and generations of the turtle tribe, sunning themselves on the fallen logs in the river. One summer, Old Jack's eighty-fourth, he spent some time planting maple saplings on his property. A year later, when I saw him dying, it seemed to me he'd meant those trees as a kind of legacy, a declaration of faith. Those of us along the river, here, won't forget him, nor what he stood for.

10   After work, I go walking and weed-inspecting. Weeds and wildflowers impress me as much as any cultivated plant. I've heard that in a year when the milkweed is plentiful, the Monarch butterflies will also be plentiful. This year the light pinkish milkweed flowers stand thick and tall, and sure enough, here are the dozens of Monarch butterflies, fluttering like dusky orange-gold angels all over the place. I can't identify as many plants as I'd like, but I'm learning. Chickweed, the ragged-leafed lambs' quarters, the purple-and-white wild phlox with its expensive-smelling free perfume, the pink and mauve wild asters, the two-toned yellow of the tiny butter-and-eggs flowers, the burnt orange of devil's paintbrush, the staunch nobility of the huge purple thistles, and, almost best of all, that long stalk covered with clusters of miniature creamy blossoms which I finally tracked down in my wildflower book — this incomparable plant bears the armorial name of the Great Mullein of the Figwort Family. It may not be the absolute prettiest of our wildflowers, but it certainly has the most stunning pedigree.

11   It is night now, and there are no lights except those of our few cottages. At sunset, an hour or so ago, I watched the sun's last flickers touching the rippling river, making it look as though some underwater world had lighted all its candles down there. Now it is dark. Dinner over, I turn out the electric lights in the cabin so I can see the stars. The black sky-dome (or perhaps skydom, like kingdom) is alive and alight.

12   Tomorrow the weekend will begin, and friends will arrive. We'll talk all day and probably half the night, and that will be good. But for now, I'm content to be alone, because loneliness is something that doesn't exist here.

READING

1. So much of description depends upon memory. How does Laurence use past and present in her essay, especially in her introduction?
2. Varying sentence length is an important element of style. How does Laurence use short and long sentences in her first paragraph?
3. Variety and similarity between sentences and within sentences is another important element of style. What principles of similarity can you discern at work in the construction of the last sentence of the first paragraph?
4. How does the author describe the river? What features does she consistently notice? What do these features contribute to the significance of the river in the essay?
5. In description, you use words to summon up physical sensations. How does Laurence summon up the trees and birds of paragraphs four and five and the weeds of paragraph ten?
6. She describes Old Jack's planting of maple saplings in his eighty-fourth summer as a "kind of legacy, a declaration of faith." What do you think she means?
7. What devices does Laurence use to give a structure to the essay as a whole?
8. Why do you think the essay is set on a Friday?

FROM READING TO WRITING

1. Remember one of your most loved places. Write down all of the things you recall about this place. Then begin to organize and structure these memories according to the patterns you perceive in them. These patterns might, for example, be spatial (organized by the physical layout of your place), temporal (organized by overlapping memories or the memory of a single moment or day), sensory (dominant smells, sights, sounds), or they might take any other form or combination of forms. Write a short essay organized and developed by these patterns.
2. Describe in journal or essay form a typical day in your life from waking up to falling asleep. Try not to use word *then* even once. Try to discover in the ordinariness of the day some patterns or significance normally hidden by ordinariness.

Robert Newman

Robert, now working on a Physics degree at the University of British Columbia, grew up in a small coastal town where there was little to do except read or write. His interests include hiking and playing piano, and he says that "writing this essay has shown me that every detail of life must be observed as important. A single blade of grass should be as clear to one's reader as a main character." He says writing teaches him "to have the patience to rewrite draft after draft without giving up ... to take something common and turn it into more, using only words."

The View from the Businessman's Corner Window

O
H, WHAT A LOVELY OFFICE! All full of mahogany and polish, the office was purchased with endless overtime and self-sacrifice. The water cooler, a gift from the president of the firm himself, glows with the rays of the noonday sun. The office is bathed in copious pools of warmth, as if the room is showing off its wonderful southern exposure. Nowhere in the building can a view be found to rival the view from the businessman's corner office window.

2   A single storey below, the cobblestones wander by, defining a wedge of waterfront park, a green and verdant space, untouched by the city's grey hand. Wizened old maples spread their gnarled shade over paths that wind in unhurried curves to the shore. A stone quay no bigger than a tennis court juts out into the bay, white sand veiling its granite footings. Endless Saharas are created and then brought to oblivion on the whims of the breeze.

3   Spring's first breeze brings riots of crocuses blazing into being, painting the earth in joyful defiance of winter's ashen majesty. With the raw bite gone from the air, dog walkers emerge towing poodles wrapped in garish hand-knit sweaters. The clicking of groomed nails slowly awakens the pavement, and the arthritic joints of the maples begin to throb with sap.

4   Returning birds flit quizzically to peer through the glass portal of the businessman's cage and then move quickly on. The sun begins to draw the

morning dew from the grass in wreaths of vapour, and a popcorn vendor arrives pushing an old and battered steam cart painted in bright reds and whites. He wanders between the dappled caves beneath the trees, with his waxed mustache and butter-stained straw boater hat. Young lovers wander the damp sand hand in hand and pass grandfathers surrounded by children sending paper navies out to meet the sunrise.

The air lies still. Overhead the summer sun rises to the zenith in a blaze 5 of heat mirage. The sweating city, baked brown, savours cold chicken and beer on ice. Aimless conversation and the clinking of glasses rise from a lazy street café.

In the centre of the park, the popcorn man peddles his wares and 6 wipes the sweat from his wrinkled forehead. He hands out paper cups of lemonade to the children dancing in the jet spray of an open fire hydrant. They weave in and out of the trees, laughing as they circle him. Notice how often the old hand forgets to collect the children's nickels.

The fleeting swirls of youth pad nimbly to the shore itself, near sun- 7 burnt swimmers embracing in the cool emerald of the ocean's grasp. A band of volleyball players claim the sand about the foot of the quay, and through the arc of their serves, sails drift by on the horizon too caught up in the freedom of the wind to pay attention to the shore.

A salty stickiness blows in off of the ocean as the day wanes into a 8 burning orange band of light and then fades slowly through ruby hues and amethyst flashes, to leave a dome of diamond-studded ebony. Below the square of light weeping from the businessman's window, a street bazaar covers the grass. The stones of the quay, radiating the heat of the day, pulsate to the rhythm of bare and dancing feet. A tarantella teases the darkness; late into the night sweet laughter trickles from the darkened corners of the summer distance.

A cool afternoon wind stirs the maples alight with autumn fire. The 9 city retreats a block, leaving the park to exhale slowly. The popcorn man shuffles through curtains of floating leaves dotted with the busy scurryings of squirrels. As the first drops of rain stain the cobbles, the popcorn man wheels his cart back into town for another year. Alone, the park beneath the businessman's window falls into slumber.

Winter blankets the world, and the sand and snow blend gentle rip- 10 ples. The harsh lines and angles of the city are softened and then erased in fog; nature's blank inevitability caresses and engulfs the sighing earth. At times, the sea seems to lie placidly, but then gales hurl it at the shore to mix with the driving rain. At times, the quay is coated in crystal from the spray that in veils rises with the wind.

Night falls so cold and still that the bay freezes into a slab of white 11 beneath the distant moon. The skeletal maples reach for the chalky orb, as if trying to escape the corpse below them.

12   The cold pall reigns as a grey eternity, choking the earth in twilight. Yet between two uneven cobbles hoared with frost, a crocus stands straight amid the patches of snow.

13   The businessman always sits with his back to the window. He likes his monolithic sepulchre of a desk to face the door, so that he can greet his visitors with a properly insincere smile. He also has a perfect view of his magnificent water cooler, a gift from the president of the firm, the president himself!

14   The water cooler's smooth symmetry is broken only by fleeting reflections of life's sweet breath tickling the panes of glass in the businessman's corner office window.

READING

1. What do the details in the introductory paragraph tell us about the businessman's relationship to his office and the view from his window?

2. How do the details of the second paragraph define the wedge of waterfront park?

3. What is the effect of the "endless Saharas" created and destroyed at the end of the second paragraph?

4. What effects does Newman use to describe the advent of spring in the third paragraph?

5. What role does the old popcorn vendor play in the essay? How does he relate to the businessman?

6. The essay describes a single space over an extended period of time. How does Newman evoke this period of time?

7. What natural devices does the author use to structure his essay?

8. Why does the essay end with the fall of winter and night?

9. What do the details in the last two paragraphs confirm about our view of the businessman?

FROM READING TO WRITING

Description is closely allied to narration. In telling a story, we naturally describe various things — scenes, people, events, etc. A description is often an indirect narration. Think of something that tells a story through its physical details. Write an essay in which you describe this thing. Do not tell the story directly. Let the details you select and the structure of the essay tell the story indirectly.

THE NARRATIVE ESSAY

NARRATION, OR STORYTELLING, has been present since prehistoric times; the people of prehistory left stories etched in stone about their daily activities. We can imagine them sitting around the fire at night, entertaining each other with stories about the hunt. Today, we engage in similar storytelling sessions around the dinner table, or at family reunions. Often our stories begin something like this: "Do you remember that time when Uncle Harold tried to start the gas barbecue and set our apple tree on fire?" The story is told and, in turn, triggers other stories in the minds of other family members.

Why do we tell stories? There are many reasons for engaging in story-telling. First of all it provides us with the opportunity to articulate the way we feel and think about our life experiences. By narrating our personal experience to another person, we can reflect on the experience and, particularly if it is a painful one, come to terms with it. On a larger scale, narratives, both oral and written, give us a sense of our culture, which in turn gives us a sense of identity.

What Is a Narrative Essay?

A narrative essay is one that tells a story, often based on the personal experience of the author. The story, or narrative, is usually told in chronological order but may also move back and forth in time. The key thing to remember when writing an essay about a personal experience is to write it in such a way that the reader is also able to find significance in the experience. As you know, experiences may be very significant for the people involved and yet hold little interest or importance for other listeners. To write about an experience so that it has meaning for your reader, you need to establish the purpose and focus of your narrative before you select and organize the elements of your story.

Giving the Narrative Essay Meaning and Focus

Perhaps the easiest way to establish a focus for your essay, thereby giving it meaning, is to write what is called an overt thesis. In any type of essay, an overt thesis is one that explicitly states the main idea or point you wish to communicate. For example, in "The Train Ride," Therese Y. Siemers directly states the thesis implied by her story or narrative of a seemingly small event that took place twenty years ago: "People still took pride in their work," she states in the last sentence of her first paragraph, "time for the little things in life, and an interest in others' feelings."

In most narrative essays, however, the meaning of an experience cannot be put into words this explicitly. Most narrative writers rely on what is called an implied thesis: one that never explicitly states the meaning of the experience. Instead, an implied thesis operates within the text of the narrative itself; the story intensifies in meaning and focus as it progresses. Readers are often not fully aware of the story's purpose until they reach the end and then reflect on the narrative. Most of the essays in this section use an implied thesis, and the meaning of the personal experience is implicitly rendered within the text of the essay.

Nancy Eng

Nancy is a University of British Columbia English major with a fond-ness for theatre, Victorian novels, and Bloom County. She finds that writing is easy when it deals with personal experiences. To write this story, she told the story on paper as if telling it to a friend. Then she returned to the work as an editor. In this way, she could concentrate on free-writing and not worry about the final product right away.

"Writing this essay reminded me that I need to have a career in the future that will provide me with enough money to eat out a lot or to hire others to cook for me, or else I may starve to death," Nancy writes.

The Importance of Cooking Dinner

1   THIS WAS NOT TO BE JUST ANY DINNER. This meal was to be a part of my rites of passage, another step into womanhood. Like the first pair of pantyhose, the first teetering steps on high heels, and the first taste of lipstick, an entire dinner prepared on one's own has always been an initiation into the adult female ranks. Despite all the advances women have made in this male-dominated world, despite the inspiration of the Sandra Day O'Connors, the Pat Carneys, and the Sally Rides, woman continues to carry certain limiting connotations. When one thinks of women, terms like *gentle, maternal,* and *domestic* still spring even to some of the most liberal minds. No matter how capable a woman is in the work world, it is still difficult to shake the time-honoured tradition of Mom baking cookies for her family, or Grandma fixing turkey for the clan. So, as I entered the kitchen that fateful day of my fifteenth year, armed with *The Joy of Cooking* and enshrouded in a "Kiss the Cook" apron, I was ready to tackle green salad, roast chicken, and chocolate mousse. I rolled up my sleeves, took a deep breath, and went to work.

2   The salad was easy enough. For that, I didn't even need to consult the cooking bible. I managed to wash and tear up a quantity of lettuce, and I threw in a variety of appropriately coloured vegetables so that my bowl more or less resembled green salad. This accomplished, I moved on with an air of confidence to the next course.

The chicken sat in all its slimy glory on a roasting pan, awaiting an 3
expert touch. Cold and slippery in my hands, it was placid and coopera-
tive as I dangled it awkwardly from one of its slick little limbs, trying to
decide which end was up. I viewed my fowl friend from several angles,
puzzled as to where exactly its head had been during its previous life. The
directions called for stuffing the animal, so I located my box of Stouffer's
Stovetop and contemplated where it belonged. Flipping the chicken
around a few more times, I finally discovered an opening. I peered into its
damp darkness, feeling slightly perverse about my actions, and hoping the
chicken didn't mind this kind of intrusion. I couldn't see how I was going
to hold that small hole open wide enough to fill the creature up, until I
spied a funnel hanging invitingly from its hook in the cupboard. Inserting
the funnel's tip into the bird, I poured in the contents of the box of stuffing, not realizing the dry, crumbly mess I was forcing in was meant to be
cooked first. The chicken soon bulged slightly with uncooked stuffing and
the innards, which I had not bothered to remove. Pleased with its bumpy
plumpness, I went on to basting.

"Butter outer chicken generously," the book directed. I partially 4
unwrapped a cold block of margarine, hoping such a substitution wouldn't
offend anyone too much, and proceeded to rub the block over the surface
of the equally cold, nubbly chicken skin with as much generosity as I
could muster toward raw poultry. Large clots of yellow stuck here and
there on the uneven epidermis, along with some bits of gold foil from the
margarine wrapper. Good enough, I thought as I flicked off some of the
larger, more conspicuous pieces of foil, time for seasoning. Nothing warms
the heart of an inexperienced cook more than a spice rack chock full of
multicoloured substances that one can sprinkle and toss with a certain
chef-like finesse. I sprinkled and tossed to my heart's content until,
inspecting my masterpiece, I discovered that I had liberally covered my
poor chicken with cinnamon, garlic powder, and sugar. Quickly, I
snapped out of my Julia Child act and remedied my mistake by attempting
to wipe off my wrongs with a paper towel. Shreds of tissue now decorated
the main course, alongside the already present foil. As dinnertime was
nearing, I tried to hurry myself along and ended up dusting the bird with
allspice, something that sounded like a good general spice to me, but
which I later discovered to be the chief flavouring for gingerbread and
apple and pumpkin pies. Being behind schedule, I didn't bother with any
more fancy stuff; I popped the chicken into the oven and cranked the
temperature up to 500° to speed up the cooking time.

Finally, it was time to prepare the dessert. A cinch, I said: no problem. 5
Setting a large pot on the burner, I began to throw in haphazardly whatever the recipe called for: squares of semisweet chocolate, cream, butter,
three separated eggs. Separated from what? I wondered; from their shells,

I guess. Happy with my conclusion, I continued, smashing the eggs along the rim of the pot, and watching the bright yellow yolks float on top of the chocolate with only a few bits of shell mixing in with them. I stirred the concoction vigorously, but it failed to resemble the light, fluffy delicacy from the glossy picture in the cookbook. Since the recipe said that this dessert was supposed to set awhile before serving, I left it on the stove, assuming it would magically take on the appearance of the cookbook picture by the time I spooned it out. Satisfied with my efforts, I left my dinner roasting and setting while I wandered off to watch *Donahue*.

6   In the middle of "Bisexual Men and Voodoo Priestesses — Compatible Marriages?" a crescendo of domestic noise swelled in my ears. The smoke alarm wailed, the oven bell clanged, and the stove crackled and sputtered. Something had gone terribly wrong. Sprinting into the kitchen, I leaped up toward the smoke alarm, waving my arms frantically in an attempt to clear the smoke and shut off the ear-piercing screech. A sharp rap with a broom handle finally silenced that contraption and allowed me to attend to what was left of dinner. The chicken was charred beyond recognition, with the bits of paper towel burning brightly and the foil glinting mockingly at me. The mousse had not transformed itself into a dessert delight that would elicit praise from my family; instead, it had melded itself to the bottom of the pot, hardening to the point where it had become an immovable part of the metal. Even my previously trouble-free salad had succumbed to the disaster surrounding it. Left sitting on the stove, the lettuce had wilted and turned an unsightly brown around its edges. As I stood in the midst of this catastrophe, in came my mother, two aunts, and my grandmother. They shook their heads sadly, and I think I actually saw tears welling up in the eyes of my grandmother. I had failed the initiation; I would never be a traditional female. No one would savour my cookies or ask for second helpings at supper. Somehow, I'd proven myself incomplete.

7   Suddenly, in the midst of this horrible, laughable affair, it dawned on me that I didn't really mind. I didn't care. This was not the be-all and end-all; I would be a woman yet. Culinary skills or not, I would amount to something. I would be one of the new breed of women who throw aside tradition to be themselves. My heart lightened. I threw off my baking mitts, untied the apron, tossed them to my grandmother, and yelled, "Call Pizza Pizza."

READING

1. In her opening paragraph, Eng contends that even the most liberal-minded people still think of women as being gentle, maternal, and domestic. Do you agree with her contention?

2. What is a rite of passage?

3. In what way has the author's attitude changed by the time she has finished preparing her distasteful dinner? Why has her dinner preparation been a liberating experience?

4. What is the significance of the title?

5. How does Eng create a humorous tone?

6. What is her thesis? Is it implied or explicit?

7. One of the most important aspects of the structure of an essay is the development of smooth and logical transitions from one paragraph to the next. For example, the author uses the transitional sentence, "This accomplished, I moved on with an air of confidence to the next course," in her move from the second paragraph, where she discusses salads, to the third paragraph, where she deals with the main course. What other examples of smooth and logical transitions can you find in this essay?

8. Does the conclusion make the essay unified? Why or why not?

FROM READING TO WRITING

1. Have you ever been through a rite of passage? How did you feel about this experience? Describe your feelings in your notebook. Then write a narrative essay based on your experience. (Your audience is someone who has been through the same rite of passage.)

Carol Geddes

Carol, a member of the Tlingit Nation, is a filmmaker and writer from the Yukon. One of her films, Doctor, Lawyer, Indian Chief, *is a National Film Board production about the struggles of Native women.*

Growing Up Native

1   I REMEMBER IT WAS COLD. We were walking through a swamp near our home in the Yukon bush. Maybe it was fall and moose-hunting season. I don't know. I think I was about four years old at the time. The muskeg was too springy to walk on, so people were taking turns carrying me — passing me from one set of arms to another. The details about where we were are vague, but the memory of those arms and the feeling of acceptance I had is one of the most vivid memories of my childhood. It didn't matter who was carrying me — there was security in every pair of arms. That response to children is typical of the native community. It's the first thing I think of when I cast my mind back to the Yukon bush, where I was born and lived with my family.

2   I was six years old when we moved out of the bush, first to Teslin, where I had a hint of the problems native people face, then to Whitehorse, where there was unimaginable racism. Eventually I moved to Ottawa and Montreal, where I further discovered that to grow up native in Canada is to feel the sting of humiliation and the boot of discrimination. But it is also to experience the enviable security of an extended family and to learn to appreciate the richness of the heritage and traditions of a culture most North Americans have never been lucky enough to know. As a filmmaker, I have tried to explore these contradictions, and our triumph over them, for the half-million aboriginals who are part of the tide of swelling independence of the First Nations today.

3   But I'm getting ahead of myself. If I'm to tell the story of what it's like to grow up native in northern Canada, I have to go back to the bush where I was born, because there's more to my story than the hurtful stereotyping that depicts Indian people as drunken welfare cases. Our area was known as 12-mile (it was 12 miles from another tiny village). There were about 40 people living there — including 25 kids, eight of them my brothers and sisters — in a sort of family compound. Each family had its own timber plank house for sleeping, and there was one large common

kitchen area with gravel on the ground and a tent frame over it. Everybody would go there and cook meals together. In summer, my grandmother always had a smudge fire going to smoke fish and tan moose hides. I can remember the cosy warmth of the fire, the smell of good food, and always having someone to talk to. We kids had built-in playmates and would spend hours running in the bush, picking berries, building rafts on the lake and playing in abandoned mink cages.

One of the people in my village tells a story about the day the old 4 lifestyle began to change. He had been away hunting in the bush for about a month. On his way back, he heard a strange sound coming from far away. He ran up to the crest of a hill, looked over the top of it and saw a bulldozer. He had never seen or heard of such a thing before and he couldn't imagine what it was. We didn't have magazines or newspapers in our village, and the people didn't know that the Alaska Highway was being built as a defence against a presumed Japanese invasion during the Second World War. That was the beginning of the end of the Teslin Tlingit people's way of life. From that moment on, nothing turned back to the way it was. Although there were employment opportunities for my father and uncles, who were young men at the time, the speed and force with which the Alaska Highway was rammed through the wilderness caused tremendous upheaval for Yukon native people.

It wasn't as though we'd never experienced change before. The 5 Tlingit Nation, which I belong to, arrived in the Yukon from the Alaskan coast around the turn of the century. They were the middlemen and women between the Russian traders and the Yukon inland Indians. The Tlingit gained power and prestige by trading European products such as metal goods and cloth for the rich and varied furs so much in fashion in Europe. The Tlingit controlled Yukon trading because they controlled the trading routes through the high mountain passes. When trading ceased to be an effective means of survival, my grandparents began raising wild mink in cages. Mink prices were really high before and during the war, but afterwards the prices went plunging down. So, although the mink pens were still there when I was a little girl, my father mainly worked on highway construction and hunted in the bush. The Yukon was then, and still is in some ways, in a transitional period — from living off the land to getting into a European wage-based economy.

As a young child, I didn't see the full extent of the upheaval. I remem- 6 ber a lot of togetherness, a lot of happiness while we lived in the bush. There's a very strong sense of family in the native community, and a fondness for children, especially young children. Even today, it's like a special form of entertainment if someone brings a baby to visit. That sense of family is the one thing that has survived all the incredible difficulties native people have had. Throughout a time of tremendous problems, the extended family system has somehow lasted, providing a strong circle for people to survive in. When parents were struggling with alcoholism or had to go away to find work, when one of the many epidemics swept through the community, or when a marriage broke up and one parent left, aunts, uncles and grandparents would try to fill those roles. It's been very important to me in terms of emotional support to be able to rely on my extended family. There are still times when such support keeps me going.

7   Life was much simpler when we lived in the bush. Although we were poor and wore the same clothes all year, we were warm enough and had plenty to eat. But even as a youngster, I began to be aware of some of the problems we would face later on. Travelling missionaries would come and impose themselves on us, for example. They'd sit at our campfire and read the Bible to us and lecture us about how we had to live a Christian life. I remember being very frightened by stories we heard about parents sending their kids away to live with white people who didn't have any children. We thought those people were mean and that if we were bad, we'd be sent away, too. Of course, that was when social workers were scooping up native children and adopting them out to white families in the south. The consequences were usually disastrous for the children who were taken away — alienation, alcoholism and suicide, among other things. I knew some of those kids. The survivors are still struggling to recover.

8   The residential schools were another source of misery for the kids. Although I didn't have to go, my brothers and sisters were there. They told stories about having their hair cut off in case they were carrying head lice, and of being forced to do hard chores without enough food to eat. They were told that the Indian culture was evil, that Indian people were bad, that their only hope was to be Christian. They had to stand up and say things like "I've found the Lord," when a teacher told them to speak. Sexual abuse was rampant in the residential school system.

9   By the time we moved to Whitehorse, I was excited about the idea of living in what I thought of as a big town. I'd had a taste of the outside world from books at school in Teslin (a town of 250 people), and I was tremendously curious about what life was like. I was hungry for experiences such as going to the circus. In fact, for a while, I was obsessed with stories and pictures about the circus, but then when I was 12 and saw my first one, I was put off by the condition and treatment of the animals.

10   Going to school in Whitehorse was a shock. The clash of native and white values was confusing and frightening. Let me tell you a story. The older boys in our community were already accomplished hunters and fishermen, but since they had to trap beaver in the spring and hunt moose in the fall, and go out trapping in the winter as well, they missed a lot of school. We were all in one classroom and some of my very large teenage cousins had to sit squeezed into little desks. These guys couldn't read very

well. We girls had been in school all along, so, of course, we were better readers. One day the teacher was trying to get one of the older boys to read. She was typical of the teachers at that time, insensitive and ignorant of cultural complexities. In an increasingly loud voice, she kept commanding him to "Read it, read it." He couldn't. He sat there completely still, but I could see that he was breaking into a sweat. The teacher then said, "Look, she can read it," and she pointed to me, indicating that I should stand up and read. For a young child to try to show up an older boy is wrong and totally contrary to native cultural values, so I refused. She told me to stand up and I did. My hands were trembling as I held my reader. She yelled at me to read and when I didn't she smashed her pointing stick on the desk to frighten me. In terror, I wet my pants. As I stood there fighting my tears of shame, she said I was disgusting and sent me home. I had to walk a long distance through the bush by myself to get home. I remember feeling this tremendous confusion, on top of my humiliation. We were always told the white teachers knew best, and so we had to do whatever they said at school. And yet I had a really strong sense of receiving mixed messages about what I was supposed to do in the community and what I was supposed to do at school.

Pretty soon I hated school. Moving to a predominately white high 11 school was even worse. We weren't allowed to join anything the white kids started. We were the butt of jokes because of our secondhand clothes and moose meat sandwiches. We were constantly being rejected. The prevailing attitude was that Indians were stupid. When it was time to make course choices in class — between typing and science, for example — they didn't even ask the native kids, they just put us all in typing. You get a really bad image of yourself in a situation like that. I bought into it. I thought we were awful. The whole experience was terribly undermining. Once, my grandmother gave me a pretty little pencil box. I walked into the classroom one day to find the word "squaw" carved on it. That night I burned it in the wood stove. I joined the tough crowd and by the time I was 15 years old, I was more likely to be leaning against the school smoking a cigarette than trying to join in. I was burned out from trying to join the system. The principal told my father there was no point in sending me back to school so, with a Grade 9 education, I started to work at a series of menial jobs.

Seven years later something happened to me that would change my 12 life forever. I had moved to Ottawa with a man and was working as a waitress in a restaurant. One day, a friend invited me to her place for coffee. While I was there, she told me she was going to university in the fall and showed me her reading list. I'll never forget the minutes that followed. I was feeling vaguely envious of her and, once again, inferior. I remember taking the paper in my hand, seeing the books on it and realizing, Oh, my God, I've read these books! It hit me like a thunderclap. I was stunned that books

I had read were being read in university. University was for white kids, not native kids. We were too stupid, we didn't have the kind of mind it took to do those things. My eyes moved down the list, and my heart started beating faster and faster as I suddenly realized I could go to university, too!

13   My partner at the time was a loving supportive man who helped me in every way. I applied to the university immediately as a mature student but when I had to write Grade 9 on the application, I was sure they'd turn me down. They didn't. I graduated five years later, earning a bachelor of arts in English and philosophy (with distinction). ...

14   Today, there's a glimmer of hope that more of us native people will overcome the obstacles that have tripped us up ever since we began sharing this land. Some say our cultures are going through a renaissance. Maybe that's true. Certainly there's a renewed interest in native dancing, acting and singing, and in other cultural traditions. Even indigenous forms of government are becoming strong again. But we can't forget that the majority of native people live in urban areas and continue to suffer from alcohol and drug abuse and the plagues of a people who have lost their culture and have become lost themselves. And the welfare system is the insidious glue that holds together the machine of oppression of native people.

15   Too many non-native people have refused to try to understand the issues behind our land claims. They make complacent pronouncements such as "Go back to your bows and arrows and fish with spears if you want aboriginal rights. If not, give it up and assimilate into white Canadian culture." I don't agree with that. We need our culture, but there's no reason why we can't preserve it and have an automatic washing machine and a holiday in Mexico, as well.

16   The time has come for native people to make our own decisions. We need to have self-government. I have no illusions that it will be smooth sailing — there will be trial and error and further struggle. And if that means crawling before we can stand up and walk, so be it. We'll have to learn through experience.

17   While we're learning, we have a lot to teach and give to the world — a holistic philosophy, a way of living with the earth, not disposing of it. It is critical that we all learn from the elders that an individual is not more important than a forest; we know that we're here to live on and with the earth, not to subdue it.

18   The wheels are in motion for a revival, for change in the way native people are taking their place in Canada. I can see that we're equipped, we have the tools to do the work. We have an enormous number of smart, talented, moral Indian people. It's thrilling to be a part of this movement.

19   Someday, when I'm an elder, I'll tell the children the stories: about the bush, about the hard times, about the renaissance, and especially about the importance of knowing your place in your nation.

READING

1. Geddes begins the essay with one of her first memories. What does this memory express about her community?

2. How does she explore and develop this image of her community in the essay? Look especially at paragraph six.

3. What are the "contradictions" she mentions in paragraph two?

4. In paragraphs four and five, Geddes discusses change and the experience of her community. How does the change in paragraph four differ from the changes in five?

5. How do you respond to the story told in paragraph ten? What do you think of the teacher's actions?

6. How does the change narrated in paragraph twelve differ from the changes discussed earlier?

7. Why do you think so much of this essay is concerned with education, with teaching and learning? Why does Geddes conclude in paragraph nineteen with a reflection on the future role of herself and her community in teaching and learning?

8. How does the author use the parallels between her individual life and the life of the Tlingit Nation to construct her essay?

FROM READING TO WRITING

1. Reflect on your own growing up. Try to recover your memories or stories of community, of growing up *something*, as Geddes grew up Native. Write a short essay narrating one of these stories fully or connecting several into a pattern suggested by the stories themselves.

Therese Y. Siemers

Born and raised in a small Alberta town, Therese moved to British Columbia after she married. Later, she returned to Alberta and became a volunteer with the LEARN adult literacy program. A graduate of Athabasca University, Therese holds both a Bachelor of Arts and a Bachelor of Education.

Therese believes that writers must have self-confidence and "dare a little." "Each essay is an experience and you have to give of yourself, your soul, to create it or it is worthless. Personal experiences make excellent material but must be well recounted to be interesting," she advises. She believes that it is essential to visualize the audience, use outlines, and be descriptive yet succinct.

The Train Ride

1   WILLOW RIVER, BC, a hamlet so small it isn't even on most road maps, is located about twenty miles from Prince George, in the heart of huge, wild forests. Twenty years ago, life was much simpler and slower paced, and a car was almost a luxury. Two cars per family was an unheard of luxury. Consequently, trains were still a central part of life, and a train ride was still an exciting treat for a 5-year-old boy. People still took pride in their work, time for the little things in life, and an interest in others' feelings.

2   Since forestry was a major industry, my husband worked in the bush, drove to camp Monday mornings, and returned on weekends. I can still picture the day I set out for the doctor's appointment, hurrying my two freshly scrubbed small sons, Benny and Dougie, over the path, through the stiff wire fence, to the tiny local whistle-stop CNR way station. This was a major undertaking with two small boys. Catching the train was a risky adventure, and it was important to arrive before the only passenger-freight train whistled by at noon. It was exciting for a small boy to rush to the edge of the elevated platform holding a red flag to signal that huge, smoking, monster diesel to a screeching, chugging, whistling stop.

3   Nattily attired in their cowboy boots and matching shirts, heads topped with cowboy hats, shoulders squared, the boys led the way. As a special treat, they were allowed to bring their own considerable earnings, which they had amassed selling pop bottles. Each had the huge sum of *one whole*

dollar. Dougie entrusted his savings to my care, but Benny proudly patted the back pocket that contained his fortune in a brand-new plastic wallet.

The boys soon got restless waiting for the train and began exploring 4 their surroundings. Through the deserted station's rooms, over the path, under the pilings, and over the railings they climbed to pass the time. Finally, the train arrived. While holding on to the railings, the boys were assisted up the steel steps by the conductor. We made our way up the long, narrow aisle to a seat. Slowly, the train started chugging on its way. Shortly thereafter, the conductor ambled down the aisle to collect my fare. As I dug into my purse for my wallet, Benny, not realizing that children under 6 travelled free, reached for his back pocket, proudly telling the conductor: "I have a dollar; I can pay for my own ticket!" To his dismay, he couldn't find the wallet. It was gone!

Slowly it sank in: the realization that he had no more wallet, no more 5 money. He was going to town and he couldn't get a treat. Bravely, Benny tried to make the best of it. He sighed: "Oh well, we can find it when we get back." Unfortunately, I had to remind him that many other children played around the train station and that his wallet was unidentified. By the time we returned on the midnight train, there would be little hope of retrieving his wallet. I was trying to console my little boy when suddenly, mysteriously, the train whistled, screeched, lurched, and came to a grinding halt.

Everybody looked around, wondering why the train had stopped. Then 6 the train started to back up. Benny looked around with mounting interest. Realization dawned. Could it be possible? Was this mile-long freight train returning to the station? Dared he hope? Would the train back up as far as the Willow River station? Was this just for him? The suspense was unbearable as the trees slowly sped by. After what seemed an interminable time, the train slowed its backward journey and crept to a halt. The door of the very car we were in stopped directly in front of the station.

Wordlessly, the same conductor who had collected the fares unhur- 7 riedly strolled down the aisle. He reached the door, turned, and slowly descended the steps, still without a word. Excitedly, Benny crept up to the door. He watched, beaming. Sure enough, the conductor was looking around the station. And there it was, the little white wallet with the Indian chief on the front, just a few steps from where Benny had boarded the train. Slowly, deliberately, and without any hint of emotion, the conductor bent down, reached out, and picked up the wallet. He climbed back on board and silently returned the hard won earnings to Benny. Still no hint of emotion crossed his face as the conductor received a big hug from the ecstatic little boy.

Silently, this anonymous stranger, this conductor who had a job to do, 8 who was responsible for keeping this passenger-freight train on schedule, made his way down the aisle: back to work, no more time for delays. But yes, something was there as he made his way down the aisle: just a hint, a ghost of a grin; the satisfaction of a job well done, which still allowed the immeasurable reward of a little boy's gratitude.

READING

1. Is the first paragraph effective in establishing the tone of the essay?

2. Who is the audience for this essay?

3. This essay is an example of a marriage of narration and description. Select some phrases, sentences, or passages that you consider to be good examples of description used in the service of narration. Indicate why you selected them.

4. What is Siemers's thesis? Is it overt or implied?

5. Do you think that the last paragraph effectively sums up the essay?

6. How do the sentences of the last paragraph express the content of the paragraph?

FROM READING TO WRITING

1. Have you made any memorable journeys? Recall a journey in which you learned something about yourself or the world. Note all the details you can recall about that event. Then, discover within these details a significant pattern, the form of your knowledge. Write an essay narrating your discovery.

Dawn Strathy

Dawn is a painter by profession and a mature student working on a Fine Arts degree at Concordia. For her, writing and painting are parallel, sister arts. Dawn finds inspiration for her writing and painting in her religion, but acknowledges that writing is "just work ... revising and revising and revising." "Perseverance," she says, "is the key word."

Incarnacion

Y OU WOULD HAVE TO BE UP before the seagulls to catch her flying   1
through narrow streets to the village market. Yet she was always
back before poor Pedro awoke. She had him washed, dressed, his
crippled body as comfortably arranged as possible in his little chair on the
street, all ready for breakfast by 7:30, just as the fishermen were returning
from their night's work, the garbageman was sounding his horn at the top
of the street, and the donkey in the villa adjoining mine had begun braying for attention. Incarnacion's day had begun. For her the same things
always happened in the same order.

She was a beautiful and talented person whom everybody loved, and   2
one of the happiest people I had ever known. From the very first day of
my painting holiday in Spain, I had been pleased to find she was my
neighbour. But I was only 23, and with the quick judgement of youth, I
had soon decided this woman's life was wasted in family drudgery. What
baffled me most of all was that she could be so happy.

Every morning the fishermen and the garbageman would greet her   3
with: "Buenos dias, Incarna!" and "Buenos dias!" she would answer, her
smile flashing. Then she would be silent a moment, looking up to the sky.
Today, years later, years in which I finally grew up, I especially remember
Incarnacion doing that, looking to the sky with always the same
inscrutable expression on her face, which I couldn't interpret then, having so little understanding. From my window I would hear and see all
these things, but I could no more read her expression than I could a
Chinese newspaper. I could only wonder, while waiting for the inevitable
cry to explode from the door behind her: "Incarnacion!" At this point
Pedro always laughed because Incarna made comical faces for his benefit
as she moved to see to the latest domestic crisis. Each day was the same
for her: it meant attending to demands of others from the beginning to

almost the end. Yet she did not give the impression of being aware of making any kind of sacrifice.

4   She had never been outside l'Escala, except once as a child when she had been taken to a bullfight in Figueras. She had hated the excursion, and from then on the people of l'Escala, the town by the sea, became her only life. She told me she had no particular desire to leave or to do anything other than what she was doing. Years before her parents had died, there had been a man in her life and a marriage had been planned, but the man had died from an attack of food poisoning. In her grief, Incarnacion had thrown herself into looking after her parents, and later, her sister's large household, especially her sister's son, Pedro. Still, she must have had lots of other marriage offers, since even when I knew her she was beautiful: apparently she had not been interested.

5   As far as I could see, she spent all her days washing, cooking, cleaning, nursing — in short, serving. She especially loved concocting herbal remedies. At night, she was often out bringing a broth or some ointment of her own concoction to a sick friend or relative.

6   I raged inwardly because I thought Incarnacion was wasting her life. She could have had a choice of careers. Besides medical talents, she had a gift for languages. If there were problems with tourists, Incarnacion translated. She was called to solve many a family crisis in the town. She was a skilled counsellor. In fact, she did just about everything well, seemingly with the greatest of ease.

7   Romantic rumours came to my ears about Incarna and the district doctor, who had never married and in whose stead Incarna was called when he was out of town. He relied on her nursing skills, and they often worked together, a fact that gave rise to cheerful gossip. Once, as we shelled peas outside my door, I asked her if she ever reconsidered marriage. From her answer it was plain even to me that when her first love died, there had been a very great and deep change in her way of looking at life. "Why not a career, then?" I asked. She hesitated, looking at me searchingly. "She's testing me," I thought. I must have failed the test because she looked up at the sky. By then I knew at least a little bit about what that meant. I had recently asked, and Incarna had told me she was not aware of doing that, but only of having little moments of prayer throughout the day. So in answer to my present question, she smiled patiently as she often did with Pedro. I knew what this meant: no more talk. She knew me pretty well, I'm afraid. I would only have argued endlessly with her, given a chance. I finally had to admit to myself that her life of devotion to others was a deliberate choice; caring for Pedro, her sister's 11-year-old spastic son, for whom nobody else had time, was her main joy. I knew I was out of my depth and could not understand such an unselfish nature as Incarna's.

The only thing I could see that she always did for herself every day 8
was to get dressed up and go out for an evening walk according to the
Spanish custom called the Hora de Paseo. First she would tidy Pedro up
and place him, as usual, in the street in his chair, hoping someone would
stop to talk to him a little. Then I would see her walking gracefully along
the streets, greeting friends as she went to see if the mail was in. Usually it
wasn't, and the broken-down bus from Figueras containing the mail, her-
alded by the shrieks of terrified pedestrians, was late careening at break-
neck speed around the corner to the post office. Waiting for the mail to
be sorted afforded Incarna a little more time to chat with friends. But she
always came back in exactly an hour to tell Pedro all the village gossip as
he ate his supper. He laughed a lot with her as one did with Incarna. His
spirit grew in her presence, and so, I now see, did mine during my times
with her. Whether Incarna was walking during the Hora de Paseo, washing a floor, or talking to Pedro, life for her always appeared to be an
adventure, though how this could be was increasingly a mystery to me. I
think she looked on me as a rather lovable but wayward child. Certainly,
as the months wore on, I grew more and more fond of her, but unfortunately our lives were soon to part, at least geographically, forever.

The last time I saw Incarna she was rehearsing the village Christmas 9
play. A child playing the part of Mary was saying the familiar words from
the Bible, "Be it unto me according to thy will." I was aware that something in my mind, heretofore dormant, began to stir. I suddenly realized
that Mary's attitude to life and Incarna's were very similar and that it
would be good if I could share their attitude, but I didn't see how I could
do that and so I dismissed the notion.

For years we exchanged Christmas cards. At some point even I real- 10
ized that life was leading me on a faith journey of my own. I wanted to
share this insight with Incarna, but I found it too hard to write about, so
instead I always chose a card with a picture of Mary on it, in the very faint
hope Incarna would get the connection and be happy that I was growing.

Then one summer, when researching an art history paper, I came 11
upon a photograph of Donatello's Unknown Prophet in a reference book.
Even though it was a poor print, it moved me very deeply. Something
about the stance and expression of the statue brought to mind Incarna
looking at the sky. I could almost hear the garbageman's horn, the returning fishermen's call, and the donkey's braying. In the reference book, I
read the words of the prophet Isaiah that art historians have associated
with the posture of Donatello's statue: "Lift up your eyes to the heavens
and consider who created it all!" Suddenly not all, but many things
became clear to me about Incarna and her importance for me. Not only
had she been a praying person, but she had had a friendly relationship
with God and with me, and I had been warmed by it. And as I read on,

"Incline your ear and come to me; hear that your soul may live," I began to see my own life in a different light. I saw that what Incarna had made of her life was unusually worthwhile and that my own life was in many ways shallow by comparison. Still, I didn't make many changes, but that year I chose my card for Incarna depicting Mary with much more care. Otherwise, I was also finding that certain words began to have more meaning for me, words like "commitment" and "availability" and "love," selfless love.

12   Finally, one Christmas a letter came from the sister saying Incarnacion had died in an accident, something to do with saving some children from being run over by the mail bus from Figueras. "That crazy bus!" and "How exactly like her," I raged, blinded by tears. But with Incarna one was never sad for long. Like Mary, she had chosen to say "Yes" to life and had drawn others along, even me. Joy returned to me. There was still pain, but I was no longer defeated by it. I often look up in the mornings now myself. I wish I had told Incarna about Donatello's statue of the *Unknown Prophet* because she would have enjoyed hearing about it and quit worrying whether I would ever grow up.

READING

1. How does the last sentence of the introductory paragraph frame the portrait of Incarnacion drawn in the opening lines?

2. Why do you think the narrator identifies herself as a painter in the second paragraph?

3. What is the significance of the distance in time and space from the subject established in the third paragraph?

4. What has Strathy come to understand about her subject that she did not understand then?

5. What parallels does the author draw between Incarnacion and the Virgin Mary?

6. In paragraph nine, Strathy speaks of Incarnacion as a mystery. Is the mystery of Incarnacion's looking up to the sky, an image introduced in the third paragraph and dramatized in the crucial incident in the seventh, explained by the reference to Donatello's statue in paragraph eleven? Or does it remain mysterious?

7. Why did the author find Incarnacion's devotion to Pedro mysterious?

8. A narrative is often a record of growth or development over time. How does Strathy use time to record her own growth?

FROM READING TO WRITING

1. Write an essay recording your growth in understanding something or someone. Begin by noting as many things as you can recall. Then try to discover a pattern in these notations. Select for the narrative the events that form a pattern and arrange them into an essay.

2. One of the crucial features of narrative is point of view. In this essay, Dawn Strathy narrates her impressions of another person from her point of view. Write an essay from another person's point of view. You can make the object of the point of view another person, place, thing, or even yourself.

Jennifer Yee

After completing her fourth year as an English major at the University of British Columbia, Jennifer is looking forward to travelling in Europe and taking time to assess her career goals. " 'Childhood Dreams' is not about myself as much as it is about how I feel about a life limited to school. I have a strong belief in living a life that includes living as well as studying," she observes.

When Jennifer writes, she reminds herself to be herself and not to think too hard. That way, her ideas flow. "Once that first word is on the page, everything begins to come out," she says.

Childhood Dreams

1   WHEN I WAS A CHILD, I loved balloons, carousels, candy floss, and my father, who shared them all with me. I never wanted more. To me, the amusement park was a place in which I was free to imagine, to indulge, even to fly. I never forgot those childhood days, but the concerns of adulthood gradually moved them to the back of my mind.

2   Sometimes, though, I dream I am at the amusement park again with my father. He takes me to the clown who sells helium balloons, each tied to a long piece of white string, and he buys me a huge red balloon. My father then ties the loose end of the string around my wrist so that the balloon does not drift away, but it does anyway, taking me with it. Grabbing a dart from one of the midway games, my father throws it at the balloon and I fall to the ground, laughing. And then we move to the carousel and he props me up on a majestic white horse with blue eyes while he rides the black one next to mine. The music starts and the horses start to trot. The tempo picks up and the horses canter. We ride through the amusement park, out into the street, along the highway, into the countryside and into the woods where gigantic trees grow. The music slows down. My father taps me on the shoulder. "Want some cotton candy?" he asks. "I'll race ya, Dad!" I scream. Then we are galloping through the trees, out of the countryside, into the city and back into the amusement park. The music stops; I wake up.

3   I forget when I last had that dream. Somewhere between my child-hood and today, I have forgotten how to laugh, how to play and how to

dream. Now, as a university student, I think about graduation, career choices, money, and marriage — not about silly balloons, carousel rides, and candy floss. As an adult, I am smothered by the real world, and no longer have the freedom to enjoy life in the same way I did when I was a child.

For example, I do not have the freedom to travel. Since starting uni- 4 versity, I have not gone on any vacations at all. No, the farthest distance I have been from Vancouver in the past four years is across the Strait to Victoria, and even that short trip gave me little feeling of freedom. Throughout the three days I spent on Vancouver Island, I felt guilty because I knew I was behind in my course reading and essay writing.

But when I do read textbooks or write essays, I am bored. Dry material 5 outlining the events of Canadian Confederation, compounded by even drier lecture material, does not inspire one to create an interesting and original essay. To examine what John A. Macdonald must have felt and thought and dreamed about Canada constitutes a far more creative essay than to detail the series of conferences at Charlottetown.

While I write a paper about the Charlottetown Conference, the 6 Quebec Conference, and the American Civil War, I pause for a moment to look out of my window, see the sunshine, and feel the warmth of a Sunday in March. I see families loading their cars with food and bad-minton sets; little girls in pigtails chasing little boys on bicycles; and my own brother and his girlfriend taking the top off his car for their drive to the Island. I look at my typewriter, questioning the importance of the British North America Act to my less-than-social life. And these are sup-posed to be the happiest days of my life? I glance at my watch — two hours before I can indulge myself with a peanut butter and jelly sandwich and a couple of carrot sticks. (I wonder what those families have in their coolers — fried chicken and potato salad?) I turn my attention back to my typewriter: B-r-i-t-

Suddenly the phone rings and I put my thoughts on hold to answer it. 7 My friend Patricia tells me that she has to cancel our lunch date on Tuesday because her boyfriend is in town and she wants to spend time with him. (I then wish that I had a boyfriend. However, I remember my last boyfriend, the one who did not understand why I spent so much time studying and so little time with him. He eventually started dating another woman.) "Hello? Are you still there?" Patricia says. I tell her to enjoy her-self with her boyfriend and then begin the goodbye rituals.

I walk back to my study. I take a photo album from my bookshelf. 8 Flipping from page to page, I see all the certificates and awards that I earned throughout my school years. I see my high-school diploma: "gradu-ated with honours standing." I sigh and look at a picture of my father that stands on the bookshelf. He always told me that school came first, that after I finished school I could find a high-paying job and then would never have to worry about money. "Yeah, Dad, after I finish school I can start my life," I think to myself.

9   I close my eyes. Let me see the balloons, the carousel, and my father with a smile on his face.

READING

1. Define what Yee means by "freedom." Support your definition with specific examples from the essay.

2. What is the thesis of this essay?

3. The daydream or reverie is used quite frequently in storytelling: think of *Alice in Wonderland* and The *Wizard of Oz*. How does the author use this technique to develop her thesis?

4. In what way does description play a central role in the development of this essay?

5. How is sentence variety used effectively in paragraph two?

6. What images in the essay conjure up a child's vision of the world?

7. How would you describe the tone of this essay? What words and expressions contribute to this tone?

8. Do you find the tone of the essay convincing? If so, what makes it work for you? If not, what would you do to change it?

FROM READING TO WRITING

1. Recall a place that was a vivid part of your childhood. Write down your memories of it in your notebook. Then, write a descriptive paragraph based on your memories. (Your audience is someone who is unfamiliar with the place.)

2. Some creative people claim that the secret to their success is keeping a connection to the child within them. Research the careers of one or more creative people — perhaps a comedian, actor, painter, scientist, or entrepreneur — and then write an essay that confirms or refutes this claim.

3

Expository Writing

An essayist is a lucky person who has found a way to discourse without being interrupted.

– Charles Poore

Look after the words, their sound, meaning, flow, cadence, and connotation, so that the sentences look after themselves.

– Laura J. Turner
(student essayist)

INTRODUCTION

I N THE SIMPLEST TERMS, exposition is the art of explaining something clearly. Exposition often answers a question of some sort. It may be something about which you are curious. For example, why do lobsters crawl backwards? How do killer bees take over other bee colonies? Or it may be a question of practical relevance. What is the best way to prepare for exams? How do various insurance schemes work, and which type is suitable for whom?

Not all exposition, though, answers an explicit question. An expository essay is any well organized piece of writing the primary purpose of which is to explain a thing, process, or idea to the reader. "Well organized" is a key phrase. Although organization is, of course, important to any type of essay, expressive writing allows the writer a great deal of leeway. You can include whatever details, images, and words you choose in a narrative or descriptive essay, as long as they capture the reader's interest and contribute to a unified whole.

However, when you are expounding or explaining, your writing must be disciplined to ensure your reader can follow your thoughts. Your thesis must be stated clearly, and your supporting points must be ordered logically so that you bring your reader along step by step. Planning and outlining are, therefore, especially important.

There is a variety of rhetorical modes, or ways to develop your explanation. In Part 3, we will look at several subcategories of the expository essay: example, process analysis, definition, comparison and contrast, analogy, and cause and effect. Of course, few essays will fit neatly into just one of these types; most essays use more than one technique, and sometimes several techniques are combined in a single essay.

EXAMPLE

P ERHAPS THE SIMPLEST and most effective method of developing an idea is to use an example. Without examples, any form of communication, be it a conversation, a speech, or an essay, can be dry and overly abstract. Examples give substance and support to your ideas, clarifying the points you are trying to make to your reader. The kinds of examples you use will depend on the purpose of your essay and on your intended reader. For instance, an essay that explains the danger of AIDS to

Example   65

high-school readers will use different kinds of examples than an essay on the same subject written for the Canadian Medical Association. Make sure your example really illustrates your point. In addition, don't use so many examples as to distract your reader from the point you are making; be selective and precise, keeping your reader in mind at all times.

Although we have placed our discussion of examples in the expository section of this book, examples are a necessary part of any type of essay. In fact, they are used by all the writers in this book. Examples take many forms, but can generally be categorized as personal experience, the experience of others, or quotations.

Personal Experience

All of the writers in Part 2 draw on their personal experience to engage the reader in their essays. In Part 3, several writers use examples from their own lives to illustrate their theses. In "Maskerade," Randal Boyd Smathers cites four incidents from his experience as a goalie to illustrate the importance of masks for all goalies. Consider, for instance, how effective and graphic Smathers's argument becomes when he includes the following example:

> I shied just twice in ten years, and suffered for it both times. The first time I flinched, I didn't see a high slapshot until it came through a screen of players. I saw the puck go back to the point, I saw the windup, I heard the shot . . . but I simply lost the puck. In such circumstances, the puck just reappears when it gets past the screen, moving toward you at an incredible speed — or seeming to, as your eyes automatically attempt to follow its flight. When the puck came straight for my eyes, it seemed to move in quantum jumps: first it was twenty feet out, then ten, and then my defence mechanism took over, and I turned my head. The puck caught a corner of my mask, and whipped through the back edge of my ear, tearing a gash that required eight stitches to close.

The Experience of Others

Another technique many writers use is to give examples from other people's lives. For example, if you were writing an essay arguing for the abolition of capital punishment, you might cite the Donald Marshall case to support your thesis. In his consideration of sports celebrities and heroes, for example, Ken Dryden cites the personal experience of Joe McGinniss:

> A few years ago, Joe McGinniss, author of The Selling of the President, 1968, wrote a book called Heroes. It sketches McGinniss's own tormented trail from being the youngest, to the highly acclaimed, to the former — all before he was thirty. At the same time, he ostensibly searches for the vanished American hero. He talks to George McGovern and Teddy Kennedy, General William

Westmoreland, John Glenn, Eugene McCarthy, author William Styron, play-wright Arthur Miller — some of them heroes of his, all of them heroes to many.

But it's like chasing a rainbow. He finds that, as he gets closer, his heroes disappear.

Quotations

Writers frequently use the words of others to support their arguments. If you use quotations in your writing, it is usually best to quote the words of an authority or of someone who is known and respected by your readers. There are two methods of integrating quotations into your essay: the first is to quote directly from the source; the second is to paraphrase the quote and integrate it into the text of your essay. All quotations and all information borrowed from somewhere else must be acknowledged. Quotations or paraphrases from written material must be properly documented. (See page 16 for more information on references.)

Elke Bittmann

Elke is a mature student who returned to school after working in the human resource field for the City of Calgary for a number of years. She works part-time while studying Sociology at Mount Royal College. She would like to do a second degree in Education. Writing has become, for Elke, a "strong focal point" and she reports that she "had forgotten how much" she enjoyed writing. The process of writing this paper reminded her of the importance of "identifying your target audience and focussing on the purpose or point or message you want to get across."

Is Happiness
Only a State of Mind?

I T'S KIND OF FUNNY, the way human society has evolved. Why, I remember, just like it was last week, when people used to struggle with life issues and when they needed help they went to their minister, parents, or friends. That, of course, was before society became dysfunctional. Our problems can now be solved for just $9.95 (Canadian, of course). 1

Many people live under the illusion that the trials and tribulations of daily life are normal occurrences. But you need only check your local bookstores to find out the truth. After reading several books you will discover that you are actually a neurotic paranoid living in a dysfunctional family, unable to get in touch with your real self. 2

Let me illustrate this point by relating the case of a close friend of mine. Susan (not her real name) had problems establishing close relationships with people she knew. In desperation she sought help at her neighbourhood bookstore. She found her help in a book titled *How to Be Your Own Best Friend*. Now she regularly takes herself out to dinner, to the movies, and to shopping malls. Of course, she did experience some uneasiness at the beginning of this new relationship, but she resolved this by purchasing the book *What to Say When You Talk to Yourself*. Susan has had no problems maintaining this relationship, since most people now give her a very wide berth when they see her. 3

Another central theme discussed in many of these books is our inability to get the things we really want (and deserve) in life. Do you want to 4 be a millionaire, an Olympic champion, or a real-estate tycoon? Or do you just want to get a parking space in front of the store? What is wrong with you? A lack of positive thinking! Yes, that is all it is — you must learn to think more positively. But positive thinking is not enough; you must also learn to visualize. You must, in your mind's eye, actually see yourself achieving the things you want to happen.

5   Let me explain my observations by relating an incident that happened to an associate of mine. My colleague (I'll call him Tony) spoke to me about his frustrations in never getting ahead. He groaned about how he was always short of money. Did he get a second job? No! Did he reduce his expenses? No! Did he consider opening a savings account? No! He went to his local bookstore to find the help he needed. He finally found the answer he was searching for.

6   Tony read many books, including *Think and Grow Rich* and *What Everyone Wants and How You Can Get It*. Tony immediately went home, sat on his sofa, and started to plan what to do with all the money he would be getting. He started to visualize his wallet filling up with hundred-dollar bills. After several weeks, Tony purchased a new car, new furniture, and new computer equipment.

7   Unfortunately, Tony must not have thought positively enough, because when the bills came in he was unable to pay them. I recently visited Tony in his new home and asked him if he thought positive thinking really worked. Tony was adamant that it did and added that he was positive he was going to be freed in the next five years and was visualizing what he was going to do after his release from prison.

8   There are many therapies and solutions advocated in all self-help books. Some of these include: confrontation techniques, where you confront the source of your problem and tell them how they ruined your life; participation in self-help groups, where you bring your self-help book and talk about how your self needs help; listening to subliminal tapes, where a message registers on your subconscious (there is some controversy about whether we actually have a subconscious, so these messages may be actually registering on your liver).

9   However, the most effective therapy I've seen is one that was shown on a local television program. This therapy was called the "Barking Therapy." I consider this one of the most effective and cheapest therapies that has ever been advocated by the television medium. To release your aggressions, stresses, and anxieties, you need only bark like a dog. For example, if you were only mildly anxious, you could bark like a dachshund — yap, yap, yap. If you suffered from severe stress, then you would bark like a German shepherd — rolf, rolf, rolf.

10   Now some people reading this will be sceptical. Does this method really work, you may ask? I can give a resounding yes, and point to the

case of Judy. Judy was waiting, waiting, and waiting for a friend. And the longer she waited, the more irritated she got. I am sure we have all experienced these frustrations at some point in our lives. But Judy decided to take control of her life and do something about it. She started barking like a terrier. And the most amazing thing happened. All the irritations and frustrations that were percolating in her stomach were forced up and released with each bark. Years of annoyances were barked away. She told me that she has now become a new person and regularly barks at anyone who gets in her way. Just imagine it — no more assaults, no more murders, no more ulcers, just a nation of people willing to lift their heads and howl at the moon.

And what about me, you may ask? What have I learned from all the *11* experiences I have shared with you? Why, I am writing a book, of course. The above dissertation and my one psychology course more than qualify me to write about my experiences and my solutions to solving the problems of society. The cost — only $9.95!

READING

1. What does "dysfunctional" mean? How does Bittmann use this word?

2. What is the tone of the first two paragraphs? At what point do you realize that Bittmann is using irony?

3. Irony could be defined as not saying directly what you mean. When you use irony, you invite your readers or listeners to reconstruct your meaning for themselves. What does Bittmann's use of irony in the first example in paragraph three allow us to understand about Susan?

4. Do the rhetorical questions of the fourth paragraph differ from those in the fifth?

5. Despite appearances, irony is almost always serious. Where does the seriousness of the author's concern begin to manifest itself?

6. Why do you think the example of Judy and her barking therapy appears last?

7. What does the author's statement about her qualifications and her (ironic) intentions in the last paragraph indicate about her purpose in writing this essay?

8. What is the actual cost, in the author's view, of these self-help programs?

FROM READING TO WRITING

1. Think of other examples of mass marketed cures, therapies, or general products of all sorts. What do these products and the marketing strategies surrounding them illustrate about us? Select several examples that share features in common, that are examples of certain trends, fashions, or developments. Write an essay, humorous or serious, ironic or direct, about these examples.

Kathleen Darlington

Writing is "plain hard work," says Kathleen. "I learned that sentences and paragraphs hardly ever fall effortlessly into place. They have to be nudged and coaxed and rewritten many times before the result feels and looks right. Once it does feel right, though, there's a great sense of accomplishment."

While her family, home, and job keep Kathleen busy, she also enjoys travel, reading, and taking courses.

Joyful William

T HERE IS A SECRET SOCIETY in every community, people who nod   1
and wave at each other in recognition. We may never know each
other's names, only the breeds of dog accompanying us on our
walks. We may, however, learn the name, sex, age, temperament, and
medical profile of the canine companion, all gleaned from snippets of
passing conversation. Most members of this society are people who develop familial relationships with their dogs, making sacrifices for them and
allowances for their misbehaviour. We are viewed by non-animal-lovers
as eccentric at best.

The many objections to having a dog in the family are valid. Messy,   2
smelly, loud, inconvenient, expensive, and time-consuming, dogs, like
children, should be carefully considered before a commitment is made.
My husband and I thought about the adjustments this new responsibility
would necessitate. We read puppy books, studied breed characteristics,
and felt we were ready for the paper training, temporary gates, and feeding
schedules. We chose to buy an Airedale terrier because they are big,
brave, loyal, intelligent, and kind to children and do not shed as much as
most dogs. We had yet to learn that they are also irrepressibly bouncy,
crafty, stubborn, and mischievous.

After choosing a breed, we still had to find a breeder with a litter, but   3
we finally found our puppy. We had to wait a whole week before we could
bring him home. During that week, we bought dishes, toys, a safety gate,
his own blanket, and a ticking clock to keep him company at night. We
named him William. He was duly and aptly registered as Joyful William.

Eight-week-old William was beautiful and lovable and insecure and   4
didn't like his ticking clock. He moved into our bedroom. This move set

the pace for his relationship with us. During the day, with everyone at work, William had to stay in the kitchen. As it took little time for him to assume the proportions of a very large Airedale puppy, he was able to reach many interesting things. We had to install child-proof cupboard latches and barricade the drawers, which he had gleefully emptied. The safety gate was replaced with a heavy door. When faced with nothing better to do, he concentrated on destroying the kitchen floor, with complete success.

5   As William matured very, very slowly, he learned proper bathroom habits and was allowed the run of the house, our theory being that he would be happier and less destructive. During the ensuing months he munched his way through a number of books, a dimmer switch he removed from the wall, and a pewter coffee set. Each onslaught was the result of our having left him alone too long. We made adjustments to the house so he would not be tempted by objects of value at doggie level. We discovered his love of soft stuffed toys, especially the ones that squeak, so he acquired a supply of bunnies and bears. We were being trained. We were becoming eccentric.

6   Friends and family began wondering aloud why we would keep such a creature. We felt like the parents of an incorrigible child, and books about dog training only encouraged the idea that we were somehow responsible for creating a monster. We enrolled in dog obedience classes. Several weeks passed, each school night worse than the one before. Going to school became an act of masochism as William became ever more creatively disobedient. I found this especially difficult since I had elected to be the handler. My husband sat on the sidelines pretending to be watching some other dog. Each week William quickly grasped his lesson at home and exhibited his profound determination not to perform at school. In shame, I admit to being a doggie-school drop-out in order to avoid the ultimate humiliation of Exam Night. I also confess to complying with William's refusal to be bullied into submission by that overbearing trainer. There were moments during class when I was almost overcome by the urge to bite her ankle on his behalf.

7   Beyond providing food, shelter, medical care, and training, part of a dog owner's responsibility involves exercise. The larger the dog, the farther he needs to walk. Large dogs who love long walks tend to enjoy being out in the most horrible weather conditions and William is no exception. We walk every night, through snow and gale force winds, thunder and rain, and below-zero temperatures. We also walk through spring mist, seeing the buds swell on trees, smelling the new, fresh life round us. We watch the seasons weave their magic through neighbourhood gardens. We walk in the heat of the summer, enjoying the pleasure of the sun on our bare arms. In autumn the evenings are cool and moonlit; fallen leaves crunch underfoot. Walking a dog with another human being creates

bonds of friendship and affection. Walking a dog alone gives one time for quiet thought.

We will never convince William to be a model dog; this clearly is not 8 to be. We have a chaotic existence of books with chomped covers, footprints on floors, noseprints on windows, and limited freedom. We also have a friend who loves us as no other.

READING

1. To what audience is Darlington directing her comments? Select at least three sentences or phrases that support your choice.

2. What is the thesis statement? Is it implied or explicit?

3. How would you describe the tone of "Joyful William"? How is this tone achieved?

4. How does the author use irony and humour to develop a captivating view on raising dogs?

5. How effective are transitions from one paragraph to the next?

6. Is sentence variety used effectively in "Joyful William"?

7. Does the conclusion sum up the thesis appropriately? Why or why not?

8. What arguments does the author provide to rationalize her love for Joyful William?

FROM READING TO WRITING

1. If you have been a pet owner, record in your notebook some of the funny or frustrating aspects of owning an animal. From your notes, write a cause and effect essay on the joys or tribulations of being a pet owner.

2. Write a process essay on the best way to train (or spoil) a dog. If you like, make your essay humorous.

Erika Ritter

Erika Ritter, born in Regina in 1948, is one of the most acclaimed of the younger generation of Canadian dramatists. Her most celebrated works are The Splits *(1978) and* Automatic Pilot *(1980).*

Bicycles

1   IT WASN'T ALWAYS LIKE THIS. There was a time in the life of the world when adults were adults, having firmly put away childish things and thrown away the key.

2   Not any more. The change must have come about innocently enough, I imagine. Modern Man learning to play nicely in the sandbox with the other grown-ups. Very low-tension stuff.

3   Now, in every direction you look, your gaze is met by the risible spectacle of adults postponing adolescence well into senility by means of adult toys: running shoes, baseball bats, roller skates, and — bicycles!

4   But the attitude is no longer the fun-loving approach of a bunch of superannuated kids and I'm sure you can envision how the evolution occurred. Jogging progressed from a casual encounter with the fresh air to an intensive relationship, attended by sixty-dollar jogging shoes and a designer sweatband. Playing baseball stopped being fun unless you had a Lacoste (as opposed to low-cost) tee-shirt in which to impress your teammates. And where was the thrill in running around a squash court unless it was with a potentially important client?

5   As for bicycles — well, let's not even talk about bicycles. On the other hand, maybe we *should* talk about them, because there's something particularly poignant about how it all went wrong for the bicycle, by what declension this once proud and carefree vehicle sank into the role of beast of burden, to bear the weight of sobersided grown-ups at their supposed sport.

6   First, there was the earliest domestication of the North American bicycle (*cyclus pedalis americanus*) in the late Hippie Scene Era of the 1960s. This was the age of the no-nuke whole-grain cyclist, who saw in the bicycle the possibility of Making a Statement while he rode. A statement about pollution, about materialism, about imperialism, about militarism, about — enough already. You get the picture: two wheels good, four wheels bad.

Thus, it was that the basic bicycle gradually evolved into a chunky   7
three-speed number from China, bowed down under a plastic kiddie carrier, army surplus knapsacks, and a faded fender-sticker advising Make
Tofu, Not War. And a rider clad in a red plaid lumber-jacket, Birkenstock
sandals, and an expression of urgent concern for all living things.

Once the very act of bicycle riding had become an act of high moral   8
purpose, it was an easy step to the next phase of the bicycle's journey
along the path of post-Meanderthal seriousness.

I'm speaking of the era of the high-strung thoroughbred bicycle,   9
whose rider had also made advances, from pedalling peacenik to a
hunched and humorless habitué of the velodrome, clad in leather-seated
shorts, white crash helmet, and fingerless gloves, whizzing soundlessly,
and with no hint of joy, down city streets and along the shoulders of
super-highways, aboard a vehicle sculpted in wisps of silver chrome. A
vehicle so overbred, in its final evolutionary stages, that it began to
resemble the mere exoskeleton of a conventional cycle, its flesh picked
away by birds of carrion.

Having been stripped of any connection with its innocent and leisure-   10
ly origins, the bicycle now no longer bore the slightest resemblance to the
happy creature it once had been. And in the mid-Plastic Scene era,
another crippling blow was struck by the upscale name-brand cyclist, who
came along to finish what the fanatical velodromist had refined. Namely,
the complete transformation of an ambling and unhurried mode of transit
into a fast, nerve-wracking, expensive, and utterly competitive display of
high speed, high technology, and high status.

The Upscale Cyclist was looking for a twelve-speed Bottecchia that   11
matches his eyes, something that he'd look trendy upon the seat of, when
riding to the office (the office!), and he was ready to pay in four figures
for it.

Not only that, he was also prepared to shell out some heavy bread for   12
those status accessories to complete the picture: the backpack designed by
the engineers at NASA, the insulated water-bottle to keep his Perrier
chilled just right, the sixteen-track Walkman that would virtually assure
him the envy of all his friends.

So much for the cyclist. What of his poor debased mount?   13

Not surprisingly, amongst the breed of bicycle, morale is currently   14
low, and personal pride all but a thing of the past. And yet ... and yet,
there are those who say that *cyclus pedalis americanus* is an indomitable
creature, and that it is the bicycle, not its rider, who will make the last
evolution of the wheel.

In fact, some theorize that the present high incidence of bicycle thiev-   15
ery, far from being evidence of crime, is actually an indication that the
modern bicycle has had enough of oppressive exploitation and man's joyless

ways, and is in the process of reverting to the wild in greater and greater numbers.

16   There have always remained a few aboriginal undomesticated bicycles — or so the theory goes — and now it is these free-spirited mavericks, down from the hills at night, who visit urban bikeracks, garages, and back porches to lure tame bicycles away with them.

17   Costly Kryptonite locks are wrenched asunder, expensive accoutrements are shrugged off, intricate gear systems are torn away, and lo — look what is revealed! Unadorned, undefiled *cyclus* in all his pristine glory, unfettered and unencumbered once more, and free to roam.

18   A wistful fantasy, you might say? The maundering illusions of someone who's been riding her bicycle too long without a crash helmet? I wonder.

19   Just the other day, there was that piece in the paper about a bicycle that went berserk in a shopping centre, smashing two display windows before it was subdued. And did you hear about the recent sighting of a whole herd of riderless bicycles, all rolling soundlessly across a park in the night?

20   It all kind of gets you to thinking. I mean, do *you* know where your ten-speed is tonight?

READING

1. What sort of tone do the first three paragraphs establish? What expectations for the essay does this tone produce in the reader?

2. Irony could briefly be defined as not saying directly what you mean or saying it in such a way as to invite your listener or reader to see the difference between what you actually say and what you may mean. How does irony work in the fifth paragraph?

3. One effect of irony is laughter. Through what short strokes of irony does Ritter create the portrait of the "Hippie Scene Era" bicyclist in paragraphs six, seven, and eight?

4. What figures or devices does Ritter use to characterize the "mid-Plastic Scene Era" of paragraphs nine to twelve?

5. How does the author begin and develop her extended metaphor of the evolutionary history of the bicycle?

6. How does the bicycle work as an example?

7. Why does Ritter use irony with this particular example? Why doesn't she say directly what the bicycle is an example of or what it demonstrates about us?

FROM READING TO WRITING

1. Think of as many contemporary trends or fashions as you can. What do they demonstrate about us? Select the trend that seems to you to be particularly demonstrative of something and write a short essay about it. Adopt the tone entirely appropriate to the trend and what you want to say about it.

Randal Boyd Smathers

An English major at the University of Alberta, Randal is pursuing a career in journalism. To relax, he heads to the Rockies to enjoy the outdoor experience.

When writing "Maskerade," Randal discovered that he enjoys the process of storytelling. He also found that editing was critical to the success of the work. "Few people have played goal in hockey, so I was describing a familiar experience — for me — to an audience with no frame of reference."

Maskerade

1   GOALIE MASKS OFTEN RESEMBLE TRIBAL TOTEMS, with weird designs painted on them, and goalies often revere them as primitive tribesmen revere their totemic symbols. Since Jacques Plante first insisted on wearing a mask in a Montreal Canadiens game on November 1, 1959, masks have prevented more injuries than any other piece of athletic equipment, and have become more important to goaltenders than anything else they own. Gerry Cheevers used to paint stitches on his mask wherever it stopped a shot, and covered his entire mask several times over. I painted my mask to match my team's colours every year — a red and black demon one year, a cubist design in gold and purple the next. My mask was a good one, a Jacques Plante special. It was made of thick fibreglass and wrapped well around my head, partially covering my ears. It was pointed in front, designed to deflect pucks away without giving them a flat surface to strike flush. My mask was more than a totem to me; it was my medicine pouch, and for good reason. The year it wore an incarnation of a blue and white hawk, it saved my sight and probably my life.

2   Due to the nature of their position, goalies have to learn to overcome their own reflexes. It is not enough that goalies allow themselves to be hit by frozen rubber pucks, weighing six ounces and moving at a hundred miles an hour, but they must not flinch even when they know a shot will hurt. This requires overcoming their bodies' own instincts against accepting pain, and some are harder to overcome than others. The hardest instinct to master is the one that turns the goalie's head away from a shot. To experience this yourself, try a simple experiment. Stand behind the net at a hockey rink sometime, and press your face up to the glass, so it

seems as if there is nothing between you and the rink; this view gives you a good imitation of the goaltender's perspective. When a shot comes straight in at your face, try not to flinch, duck, or blink; that's the test a goalie faces a dozen times a season. You need practice to let the puck hit the glass in front of you, but even more so when the puck hits your mask, driving it back into your skull as if you've just been hit with a baseball bat. Normally, goalies have time to duck under a high shot, but when they don't, they can't afford to turn away. Like army tanks, goal masks are meant to be hit from the front, where their protection is the greatest, and where shots deflect without hitting squarely.

I shied just twice in ten years, and suffered for it both times. The first 3 time I flinched, I didn't see a high slapshot until it came through a screen of players. I saw the puck go back to the point, I saw the windup, I heard the shot ... but I simply lost the puck. In such circumstances, the puck just reappears when it gets past the screen, moving toward you at an incredible speed — or seeming to, as your eyes automatically attempt to follow its flight. When the puck came straight for my eyes, it seemed to move in quantum jumps first it was twenty feet out, then ten, and then my defence mechanism took over, and I turned my head. The puck caught a corner of my mask, and whipped through the back edge of my ear, tearing a gash that required eight stitches to close.

The second time I shied was worse. Again it was a high slapshot com- 4 ing in from the blueline, and again I was tensed and ready for the impact, but this time a stick reached out from a thicket of players about ten feet in front of me and just barely touched the puck. Normally, on such a close-in deflection, a goalie would have no time to move at all, but because the puck was suddenly angled right at my face, I had a marvellously clear view of its approach. Again, at the very last, my head jerked sideways involuntarily. Unfortunately, it also jerked upwards, and the puck just caught the bottom edge of my mask and smashed downward into my throat. I was lucky enough not to suffer any permanent damage, but lying on the ice and gasping for breath, I felt sure that my larynx had been crushed. Every breath for the next two weeks was painful, and I ate no solids in that time, but I had learned my lesson: never turn my head.

I didn't learn that lesson too soon, because the next year I took the 5 worst shot of my career. It happened in a pregame warmup. Warmups are supposed to get the goalie ready to play, but they frequently turn into target practice for the rest of the team. On this day, a puck was lying about fifteen feet in front of the net. One of the team's best players, a big farm boy with forearms like Christmas hams, came charging in for the puck. Coasting the last five feet, he reached well forward with his stick, pulled the puck back behind him, cradled it in the curve of the blade, and bent his full weight onto the shaft. I never really saw the shot. What I did see was the puck, completely filling the right eyehole of the mask: the puck came too fast for comprehension at such short range. I'm told it was funny to watch — first I dropped to my knees, then I swayed forward, then I went right over backwards into the net. All I remember is coming to, looking up at the crossbar of the goal. My mask, which connected to its straps by five snaps so tightly I closed them with a hammer, was behind the net. The puck, rising and still accelerating when it struck me, had hit the top of the eyehole, ripped the mask off my face by popping loose all the snaps except the one high on the centre of my forehead, and blown the mask over the back of the net. I came out of that with a headache that a couple of Anacin cured, played the rest of the game (the defence gave me a lot more support than usual), and discovered a new respect for my mask, which suffered not even a chip.

6   I had played only one game without a mask — something completely against the rules — when I went for a road game and left it behind. My mother drove like a madwoman back to our house, about fifteen miles each way, to fetch my mask, and in the meantime I just went without one. The other team promised not to shoot over my waist. I remember one scene from that game vividly. As a short goalie, I was susceptible to screening. Early in my career I had learned to beat a screen by spreading my legs about four feet apart, and bending at the knees and waist until my chin was no more than six inches off the ice. By doing this, and then bobbing and ducking from side to side, I could usually follow the movement of the puck through the skates, legs, and sticks. While I was playing without a mask, I suddenly found myself in my familiar position, trying to spot the puck behind a few bodies. It occurred to me that I had to be a damn fool to do this, standing with my unprotected face down where it was most vulnerable to shots, sticks, and skates, and so I spent the rest of the time until my mask arrived standing on tiptoe, trying to see over players.

7   I came out of that season with a new appreciation for the goalies who played without masks, before and after Plante in 1959, although I have to seriously question their sanity. I also consider it a miracle that no goalie ever died before masks were invented. After another season, I was forced by my need for glasses to wear a cage mask, but I have never let go of my Jacques Plante special, and I never did get around to painting over the big black rubber smear over the right eyehole.

READING

1. What is the significance of Smathers's decision to alter the spelling of Masquerade?

2. Do you think that his comparison of a goalie's mask to a tribal totem is appropriate and effective? Why or why not?

3. What are important features in the design of a goalie's mask?

4. What instincts or reflexes do goalies have to overcome? How many examples does the essay give of the results of giving in to them?

5. Who is the intended audience?

6. Do you think Smathers is proud of his abilities to play goal? Why or why not?

7. One of the author's writing strengths is his ability to give a goalie's eye view of a hockey game and, in particular, an oncoming puck. Select the paragraph you think is most effective and explain your choice.

8. A well written opening paragraph should capture the reader's attention and clearly introduce the topic of the essay. Does this essay succeed on both counts? How?

9. Does the concluding paragraph summarize the essay and reinforce its content? Why or why not?

FROM READING TO WRITING

1. Recall an exciting moment in a game you played. Make notes on how you felt, what you saw, how you and the other player(s) moved. Describe the skills you needed and the view you had of the game from your position. Write the descriptive essay that has developed through your notes.

2. Hockey players, especially goalies, wear several layers and types of protective gear. Hockey is a rough game. Which is the cause and which is the effect? That is, do the players wear so much protection because the game is rough, or do they tend to play roughly because they are so well protected? Consider some games you have played or witnessed. Write a short argument essay defending your thesis.

PROCESS

HAVE YOU EVER NOTICED the number of books and magazines that offer advice on our health, houses, gardens, wardrobes, relationships, thighs, face, and hair? This kind of writing explains how to achieve a goal, often through step-by-step instructions. Like these books and magazine articles, a process essay explains to its readers either how to perform a task or how something works.

In writing the process essay, always keep two things in mind: your purpose and your reader. Although considering your reader is important for every type of essay, in process writing it is absolutely essential. Since the goal of a process essay is to enable your readers to accomplish a task or understand how something works, you must continually ask yourself what they already know and what they need to be told. Consider for a moment the lost strangers who stop you on the street for directions. Unless you find out exactly how much they know of the area, you are likely to lead them further astray. Similarly, a process essay will lose your readers unless you determine their level of knowledge before you begin the essay. Thus, a process essay on kitchen renovation for the layperson will be different from an essay on the same subject written for an architect.

Eileen A. Brett

Eileen, currently a student at the University of British Columbia, enjoys sports (from softball to ultra-light flying), playing the flute, and sewing. She also enjoys reading because it enables her to discover more about the world and about how people think. She finds that her writing is most effective when it is natural, rather than pressured. "When you write, just be yourself. Don't imitate someone else's style; let your own personality come through," Eileen recommends.

How to Write a Test

I T IS THE DAY OF THE FINAL EXAM or perhaps it is just a unit quiz. (Of 1 course, in today's academic courses, when entire grades are sometimes comprised of quiz marks, there is no such thing as a mere quiz.) Whether quiz, test, or examination, does the very suggestion of being tested induce fear and panic? Rest assured; writing tests need not be a frightening experience. If you sit in a place without distractions, bring the right tools, relax, think positively, and organize yourself, you will survive the experience. You may even surprise yourself by doing well on the test.

As you enter the classroom the day of the test, your first priority 2 should be to choose where to sit. The important point here is not to find the most comfortable seat but to avoid windows. When a task of importance is unpleasant, eyes tend to wander toward windows and scenes of interest outside. When this happens, inevitably, concentration is relaxed. Equally distracting can be a seat at the back of the room where the back view of any number of attractive blondes or rugged athletes will be in your direct line of vision. Always choose a seat in the front row.

To be prepared you will have brought with you at least two pens and 3 one pencil accompanied by a bottle of correction fluid, an eraser, and a watch. Often I have forgotten this last item and suffered tremendously from judging incorrectly how much time remained. These are the essential tools of any test. The pencil may be used substantially more than the pen, for reasons that will be discussed later. One pencil is sufficient, since the walk to the pencil sharpener provides a practical excuse to exercise leg muscles. I stress, however, that this is not an opportunity to cheat. The walk over to the pencil sharpener is not only a form of physical release, it is also a "brain break." However short this walk may be, the brain welcomes the chance to escape deep mental concentration for the non-strenuous act of sharpening a pencil.

4   Many students spend the remaining few minutes before the test cramming crucial bits of information into their heads. This effort is wasteful since, in my experience, last minute cramming serves to confuse and is not actually remembered anyway. Why not, instead, spend those moments in mental relaxation and deep breathing? At the same time, analyze the mood in the room. If absolutely everyone else, not having read these helpful hints, is deeply engrossed in last minute preparation, this is a fairly positive indication that the exam will be a difficult one. In this case, it is best that you breathe deeply rather than analyze. If, on the other hand, the majority is calm, cool, and collected, either the test is going to be easy or you have got the date wrong. In both cases, you have nothing to worry about.

5   The interval between the time the test is placed in front of you and the time you are told you may begin is the time to take the Attitude Adjustment Approach, which concerns the mindset in which you will commence writing the exam. During this time, students who want only to scrape by will decide to put minimum effort into the exam. In contrast, students who want a good, if not exceptional, grade will use this time to prepare mentally for the challenge ahead.

6   As the examination begins, take a moment to glance through the test. The decision as to where to start is yours. However, a word to the wise: multiple choice questions should be attacked first for two reasons. First, tidbits of information can often be gleaned from them and then reworked to fit nicely (and inconspicuously) into sentence answers or essays. Second, since the answer is right in front of you, multiple choice questions are the least painful way of easing into the task ahead.

7   In examinations, an organized student has the advantage over a disorganized student. An organized system for writing tests involves using a pen or pencil, depending on how confident you are with the material. Those answers of which you are fairly certain should be answered in pen. Otherwise, pencils are ideal for answering tests because answers can be changed easily. However, since numerous studies have found that, particularly with multiple choice, the first answer chosen is most often the correct one, be 110 percent sure before you change an answer. Should time permit double-checking, it will be necessary to review only those answers in pencil as answers in pen are likely to be correct. If an answer is elusive, make a mark beside the question so you will be able to quickly identify those questions to which you did not know the answers. Then move on and go back to them later.

8   A few techniques have been developed for writing essays. Of course, understanding exactly what the question is asking is essential. If, for

example, there is more than one essay question, ideas may flow more freely if you switch back and forth among them. When I begin to get frustrated for lack of ideas, often new thoughts will surface as I answer another question and I will quickly jot them down. Still, other people find staying with one essay until it is completed more beneficial. If all else fails, use the technique of free-writing: write on anything that is even remotely connected with the essay topic until you feel inspired. But perhaps you should take a brain break.

The technique you choose is of less importance, though, than the   9 interest level of your essays. Not many teachers enjoy perusing forty essay exams on "The Effect of Green Pesticides on Small Herbivores." If you want a good mark, you will strive to keep the professor not only awake but also excited at your discussion of genetic differences in field mice. Imagination is a wonderful asset, but if it is not one of yours, description or examples are also effective. Easy reading is also enhanced by grammatically correct writing.

Before you finish the exam, remember to finish those multiple choice 10 questions that you had found impossible to answer. If the process of elimination does not yield an answer that is satisfactory, depending on the amount of time remaining, one of two options is open: count up how many A answers you have, how many B, etc., and choose the letter that has the least number of answers; or take a reasonable guess. If all else fails, write your professor a note telling him or her of the immense satisfaction and enjoyment you derived from doing the exam, and extend holiday greetings. Then, with hope, you wait for the results and you trust that:

(a) Without your knowledge, your teacher has sent in several of your essays from the examination to Mensa, which extends the honour of membership to you.

(b) The test was for the government, which does not care anyway.

(c) The teacher appreciated your note.

READING

1. According to Brett, what are the components of an examination?
2. In point form, note the suggestions she gives for success on exams.
3. What does the author mean by the "Attitude Adjustment Approach"?
4. Which of her strategies do you think is the most helpful and effective? Why?

5. Do you disagree with any of her strategies? If so, which one(s) and why? Which strategies of your own would you add to the process?

6. Do you find the conclusion of the essay effective? Why or why not?

7. Note the author's use of humour. Select some examples you find particularly amusing, or some examples of humour that fall flat for you. Explain your choices.

8. Do you think she uses humour to enhance her thesis? Explain your answer.

FROM READING TO WRITING

1. Work up an outline explaining a school-related process at which you are an expert. You might, for example, discuss one of the following:

   (a)   How to get an *A* in a course.

   (b)   How to con a teacher.

   (c)   How to guarantee a perfect class schedule.

   Feel free to choose your own topic. Then develop the outline into a well organized essay.

2. Why do some people have difficulties writing a successful test? Conduct some research in the library on exam anxiety. Then write either a cause and effect essay citing three reasons for exam anxiety or a process essay suggesting three ways to overcome exam anxiety. (Your audience is someone who wants to overcome the problem.)

Donald M. Murray

Donald M. Murray won a Pulitzer Prize in 1954 for his editorials in the Boston Herald. *He worked as an editor with* Time *magazine before accepting a position at the University of New Hampshire. The following essay appeared in 1973.*

The Maker's Eye: Revising Your Own Manuscripts

WHEN STUDENTS COMPLETE A FIRST DRAFT, they consider the job 1 of writing done — and their teachers too often agree. When professional writers complete a first draft, they usually feel that they are at the start of the writing process. When a draft is completed, the job of writing can begin.

That difference in attitude is the difference between amateur and pro- 2 fessional, inexperience and experience, journeyman and craftsman. Peter F. Drucker, the prolific business writer, calls his first draft "the zero draft" — after that he can start counting. Most writers share the feeling that the first draft, and all of those which follow, are opportunities to discover what they have to say and how best they can say it.

To produce a progression of drafts, each of which says more and says 3 it more clearly, the writer has to develop a special kind of reading skill. In school we are taught to decode what appears on the page as finished writing. Writers, however, face a different category of possibility and responsibility when they read their own drafts. To them the words on the page are never finished. Each can be changed and rearranged, can set off a chain reaction of confusion or clarified meaning. This is a different kind of reading which is possibly more difficult and certainly more exciting.

Writers must learn to be their own best enemy. They must accept the 4 criticism of others and be suspicious of it; they must accept the praise of others and be even more suspicious of it. Writers cannot depend on others. They must detach themselves from their own pages so that they can apply both their caring and their craft to their own work.

Such detachment is not easy. Science fiction writer Ray Bradbury sup- 5 posedly puts each manuscript away for a year to the day and then rereads it as a stranger. Not many writers have the discipline or the time to do this. We must read when our judgment may be at its worst, when we are close to the euphoric moment of creation.

6   Then the writer, counsels novelist Nancy Hale, "should be critical of everything that seems to him most delightful in his style. He should excise what he most admires, because he wouldn't thus admire it if he weren't … in a sense protecting it from criticism." John Ciardi, the poet, adds, "The last act of the writing must be to become one's own reader. It is, I suppose, a schizophrenic process, to begin passionately and to end critically, to begin hot and to end cold; and, more important, to be passion-hot and critic-cold at the same time."

7   Most people think that the principal problem is that writers are too proud of what they have written. Actually, a greater problem for most professional writers is one shared by the majority of students. They are overly critical, think everything is dreadful, tear up page after page, never complete a draft, see the task as hopeless.

8   The writer must learn to read critically but constructively, to cut what is bad, to reveal what is good. Eleanor Estes, the children's book author, explains: "The writer must survey his work critically, coolly, as though he were a stranger to it. He must be willing to prune, expertly and hard-heartedly. At the end of each revision, a manuscript may look … worked over, torn apart, pinned together, added to, deleted from, words changed and words changed back. Yet the book must maintain its original freshness and spontaneity."

9   Most readers underestimate the amount of rewriting it usually takes to produce spontaneous reading. This is a great disadvantage to the student writer, who sees only a finished product and never watches the craftsman who takes the necessary step back, studies the work carefully, returns to the task, steps back, returns, steps back, again and again. Anthony Burgess, one of the most prolific writers in the English-speaking world, admits, "I might revise a page twenty times." Roald Dahl, the popular children's writer, states, "By the time I'm nearing the end of a story, the first part will have been reread and altered and corrected at least 150 times. … Good writing is essentially rewriting. I am positive of this."

10   Rewriting isn't virtuous. It isn't something that ought to be done. It is simply something that most writers find they have to do to discover what they have to say and how to say it. It is a condition of the writer's life.

11   There are, however, a few writers who do little formal rewriting, primarily because they have the capacity and experience to create and review a large number of invisible drafts in their minds before they approach the page. And some writers slowly produce finished pages, performing all the tasks of revision simultaneously, page by page, rather than

draft by draft. But it is still possible to see the sequence followed by most writers most of the time in rereading their own work.

Most writers scan their drafts first, reading as quickly as possible to 12 catch the larger problems of subject and form, then move in closer and closer as they read and write, reread and rewrite.

The first thing writers look for in their drafts is *information*. They 13 know that a good piece of writing is built from specific, accurate, and interesting information. The writer must have an abundance of information from which to construct a readable piece of writing.

Next writers look for *meaning* in the information. The specifics must 14 build to a pattern of significance. Each piece of specific information must carry the reader toward meaning.

Writers reading their own drafts are aware of *audience*. They put 15 themselves in the reader's situation and make sure that they deliver information which a reader wants to know or needs to know in a manner which is easily digested. Writers try to be sure that they anticipate and answer the questions a critical reader will ask when reading the piece of writing.

Writers make sure that the *form* is appropriate to the subject and the 16 audience. Form, or genre, is the vehicle which carries meaning to the reader, but form cannot be selected until the writer has adequate information to discover its significance and an audience which needs or wants that meaning.

Once writers are sure the form is appropriate, they must then look at 17 the *structure*, the order of what they have written. Good writing is built on a solid framework of logic, argument, narrative, or motivation which runs through the entire piece of writing and holds it together. This is the time when many writers find it most effective to outline as a way of visualizing the hidden spine by which the piece of writing is supported.

The element on which writers may spend a majority of their time is 18 *development*. Each section of a piece of writing must be adequately developed. It must give readers enough information so that they are satisfied. How much information is enough? That's as difficult as asking how much garlic belongs in a salad. It must be done to taste, but most beginning writers underdevelop, underestimating the reader's hunger for information.

As writers solve development problems, they often have to consider 19 questions of *dimension*. There must be a pleasing and effective proportion among all the parts of the piece of writing. There is a continual process of subtracting and adding to keep the piece of writing in balance.

Finally, writers have to listen to their own voices. *Voice* is the force 20 which drives a piece of writing forward. It is an expression of the writer's authority and concern. It is what is between the words on the page, what glues the piece of writing together. A good piece of writing is always marked by a consistent, individual voice.

21   As writers read and reread, write and rewrite, they move closer and closer to the page until they are doing line-by-line editing. Writers read their own pages with infinite care. Each sentence, each line, each clause, each phrase, each word, each mark of punctuation, each section of white space between the type has to contribute to the clarification of meaning.

22   Slowly the writer moves from word to word, looking through language to see the subject. As a word is changed, cut, or added, as a construction is rearranged, all the words used before that moment and all those that follow that moment must be considered and reconsidered.

23   Writers often read aloud at this stage of the editing process, muttering or whispering to themselves, calling on the ear's experience with language. Does this sound right — or that? Writers edit, shifting back and forth from eye to page to ear to page. I find I must do this careful editing in short runs, no more than fifteen or twenty minutes at a stretch, or I become too kind with myself. I begin to see what I hope is on the page, not what actually is on the page.

24   This sounds tedious if you haven't done it, but actually it is fun. Making something right is immensely satisfying, for writers begin to learn what they are writing about by writing. Language leads them to meaning, and there is the joy of discovery, of understanding, of making meaning clear as the writer employs the technical skills of language.

25   Words have double meanings, even triple and quadruple meanings. Each word has its own potential for connotation and denotation. And when writers rub one word against the other, they are often rewarded with a sudden insight, an unexpected clarification.

26   The maker's eye moves back and forth from word to phrase to sentence to paragraph to sentence to phrase to word. The maker's eye sees the need for variety and balance, for a firmer structure, for a more appropriate form. It peers into the interior of the paragraph, looking for coherence, unity, and emphasis, which make meaning clear.

27   I learned something about this process when my first bifocals were prescribed. I had ordered a larger section of the reading portion of the glass because of my work, but even so, I could not contain my eyes within this new limit of vision. And I still find myself taking off my glasses and bending my nose towards the page, for my eyes unconsciously flick back and forth across the page, back to another page, forward to still another, as I try to see each evolving line in relation to every other line.

28   When does this process end? Most writers agree with the great Russian writer Tolstoy, who said, "I scarcely ever reread my published writings, if by chance I come across a page, it always strikes me: all this must be rewritten; this is how I should have written it."

The maker's eye is never satisfied, for each word has the potential to 29
ignite new meaning. This article has been twice written all the way through
the writing process, and it was published four years ago. Now it is to be
republished in a book. The editors made a few small suggestions, and then
I read it with my maker's eye. Now it has been re-edited, re-revised, re-read,
re-re-edited, for each piece of writing is full of potential and alternatives. 30
     A piece of writing is never finished. It is delivered to a deadline, torn
out of the typewriter on demand, sent off with a sense of accomplishment
and shame and pride and frustration. If only there were a couple more
days, time for just another run at it, perhaps then ...

READING

1. What differences and similarities does Murray see between professional writers and student writers? Are there more similarities or
   differences?
2. How does the author use the sentences of the introductory paragraph to express these similarities and differences?
3. How does the kind of reading he argues writers must practise differ
   from the reading he claims we learned in school (see paragraph
   three)?
4. What is the relation between the kind of reading he discusses and
   the process of rewriting?
5. What do you think he means in paragraphs eighteen and nineteen
   by "development" and "dimension" in writing?
6. Murray observes in paragraph 24 that "making something right is
   immensely satisfying, for writers begin to learn what they are writing about by writing." Writing about something obviously involves
   learning about that thing. But do you think that writing is in itself a
   learning process? How so?
7. How is the metaphor of the maker's eye developed in the anecdote of the bifocals in paragraph 27?
8. Do you find that Murray's analysis of the process of writing describes
   your own experience? How do you experience the writing process?

FROM READING TO WRITING

1. Recall the process involved in writing your last essay or any other
   piece of writing that gave you great pleasure or pain. Recall each

stage of the development of your writing, each evolution of the dimensions of that piece of work. See if you can create a central metaphor to illustrate your experience of the process. Then write a short process analysis using the central metaphor.

2. So many of the physical things we do each day we take for granted. But when we stop to analyze them or, for various reasons, have difficulty doing them ourselves, we realize how complex they can be and perhaps appreciate how difficult they may be for others. Write an essay analyzing and explaining the process of any commonplace everyday event like tying your shoes, driving a car, making a telephone call, typing a letter, doing the laundry, etc.

Patricia Schmida

Patricia and her husband, whom she describes as "the best friend I could ever imagine," attend the University of Ottawa. Patricia hopes to become a research psychologist and writer. Although she finds making time for her writing a struggle, and writing itself sometimes "slow-going and painful," she says that in writing this essay she learned at least one valuable lesson: "I learned to trust my own voice."

Self-Analysis Through Dream Exploration

PSYCHIATRY. PSYCHOLOGY. THERAPY. Still here? Why do these words *1*
make many of us turn away or change the subject? Let's try something else. Happiness. Success. Love. Freedom. Any of these sound appealing? For some, the first and second lists have nothing in common. For others they are directly linked. Which are they for you?

If you know that there are some areas you would like to work on, but *2*
therapy is an ugly word for you, don't despair. No one may have told you this before, but you have your very own built-in therapist, right inside your brain. Like the earth, like a spider's legs or bird's broken wing, like everything else in nature, human beings have the constant ability for self-healing and damage repair. For instance, our body maintains its homeostasis through signalling its needs to us through urges: we feel hungry when our sugar levels are low: thirst signals dehydration. But the needs of the human being are not always physical. Much like the physical ones, our emotional needs make themselves known too. One way is through our dreams.

Have you ever woken up from an incredibly erotic dream and won- *3*
dered, where did that come from? Or have you suffered through the treachery of a nightmare? Maybe you have remembered bizarre snippets of dreams when you have woken up and puzzled over their significance only to find they have disappeared a moment later. Or perhaps the snippets were either uncomfortably disconcerting or else profoundly pleasurable, and then lingered on in the very back corner of your memory all day.

Your dreams are actually telling you more about yourself than any other *4*
person in your life ever could. You might talk for hours with confidants, read every self-help book on the shelf, and try every form of stress-release

out there, including exercise, meditation, weekend retreats, inner exploration workshops, or ten-step programs — but there is a much easier way.

5   Becoming your own dream analyst is simple and exciting. All you
need is a blank notebook, a pen, and an open mind. Make sure to choose
a notebook that you will use specifically for the purpose of dream analysis.
You may want to find a special book with a visually pleasing cover, or you
may take a plain notebook and decorate the cover with cut-out pictures,
wrapping paper, photos, markers, or whatever you find attractive. Take
pride in your book.

6   Dream analysis begins before the dream even occurs. You can start
tonight. In the evening, if you do not already, allow yourself some time
(the longer the better, but at least fifteen minutes) to wind down from
your day. Forget both your professional and personal life. Relax by enjoying a cup of tea, reading, or simply lying in bed comfortably and thinking
— do whatever works best for you. Removing your self from your day
allows you to reflect on it more clearly. Now take your dream book in
hand, and write the date, and then capture the day. Write what you did,
what happened to you, and how you felt about it. Write in point form to
conserve space and time. Try to single out which events held significance
for you today. Was there something that made you feel proud, a moment
of sadness, a pleasurable exchange with a co-worker, friend, or relative, or
was there discouraging news; was there a wish for your future, a moment
of laughter, a moving sunset, a disturbing movie, or a goal realized? Let
your mind retrace the day from beginning to end, and try to write everything that mattered and nothing that did not. Here is an example:

- woke up feeling really good for some reason
- ran into old high-school friend, felt excited but strange too
- boring day at work, but did get a lot done — felt proud
- feeling more tired than usual tonight
- invited parents for dinner next Saturday

When you are satisfied with what you've written, draw a line under it. This
line ends all conscious thoughts of the day. Now it is time to allow the
subconscious to sort through it all for you. In fact, if you are experiencing
any confusion or indecision over something in your life, ask the question
at the end of your list. "Why am I so self-critical?" Or "Should I date Chris?"
Or "What's missing from my life? What would make me happy?"

7   All of this self-reflection may seem difficult at first, or it may come
naturally to you and only writing it all down is new. Dream analysis offers
almost immediate benefits, though, so stick it out until it becomes a
comfortable and normal part of your life.

Keep your notebook right beside your bed, or as near as possible. 8
When you awake in the morning, reach for it first thing. Capture as
much of your dream as you can, quickly, by writing down key words and
feelings. The notes do not have to make any sense at all. If you don't
remember your dream, write down how you slept and how you feel now.
With dream analysis, practice will make perfect. The more you are willing to pay attention to the world inside of you, the more it will be willing
to share itself.

After you have written down your dream, draw a line across the page, 9
which signals your mind to leave the dream and carry on with your day.
Also you have left your dream book ready for tonight when you will start
the cycle fresh again. You don't need to dwell on your dreams for hours to
learn from them. In fact, the less time spent reflecting on them daily, the
better. What you need now, to complete the process of dream analysis, is
a weekly time set aside for the actual analysis. This analysis is best accomplished when you have the most time for yourself, whether Sunday afternoon or Wednesday morning.

The actual analyzing is both the most challenging and the most 10
rewarding aspect of dream analysis. This skill takes time to develop. Once
a week for about 30 minutes is about the right amount of time to spend on
this step. Read through the week's entries, following chronologically from
day to dream to day. Look for patterns and associations. Pay close attention to repetitive symbols in dreams, for instance: doors that won't lock,
monsters, flowers, drowning in water, or eating ice cream. We are all
unique, and we have all had unique lives. Only you can decipher your
symbols. Tied to each symbol is usually an emotion. Take either that feeling or the symbol itself and concentrate on your past memories. What did
ice cream mean as a child? Was it a reward, or a way to divert/reject me?
What did my backyard mean to me, freedom or confinement? and then —
who is rejecting me now? What is offering me freedom? When did I feel
confined this week? If this process seems confusing, here is a simple step-
by-step method. From your dream, gather up the key objects, people,
places, etc., and list them in your book. Next, go through each thing one
by one. Concentrate on what this object has meant to you in the past. If
you dreamt of your mother, ask yourself, what is a mother? How do I feel
about mothers in general, and how do I feel about mine? If you dreamt of
a monster, ask yourself, what is a monster? You are not looking for dictionary definitions. You want to learn about your own meanings behind the
symbols your subconscious uses. Gradually you can build your own com-
prehensive dictionary of symbols, one that is unique to you.

Although most symbols will be your own creations, some symbols 11
seem common to many dreamers. For instance, a scary entity that is chasing you in a dream is probably an unexpressed part of you. Remember,

your whole dream is you, because you created it. Maybe in real life you have trouble expressing certain parts of your personality, for instance anger or assertion; therefore, you express them in the dream. Another example of a common activity in dreams is a descent downward, perhaps in an elevator or on an escalator, or maybe down a hill. This descent often represents your own accessing of deeper levels of your subconscious where repressed fears and desires are hidden. The more you pay attention to these, the more they will tell you. Another common occurrence is to dream of babies or giving birth. A baby is often a symbol of a new part of yourself being born. This birth can be a real inspiration to you and give you a profound sense of renewal and power. If you are interested in discovering other common dream symbols and patterns, you can consult psychology books in the library. But here is the straightforward truth: dream analysis truly works best in conjunction with therapy. The simple fact of the matter is a psychiatric doctor is trained to decode this wonderful mysterious world of the subconscious in ways that we simply don't learn. The doctor acts as a guide and as a reference for you. But, of course, professional therapy is far from necessary for you to learn from your dreams. You can work wonders on your own too.

12   These recordings of day and night are pieces of a puzzle that will fit. But you need patience and desire. If you are willing to spend effort on becoming more self-aware through dream analysis, you can reap uncountable rewards. You can learn to answer your own questions and understand your own feelings. You can begin to identify and accept your needs as natural parts of yourself. And finally, you can gain some understanding and direction toward what it would take to make you feel good about yourself and good about the world you create for yourself. Understanding your dreams could be the first step in making your dreams come true.

READING

1. Do you find that the rhetorical questions work well as an introduction?

2. What is the physical process of homeostasis mentioned in the second paragraph and how does it relate to dreams?

3. Where does Schmida move to the actual process of analysis?

4. What are the steps in the process of dream analysis?

5. Why do you think the author does not analyze her own dreams but instead instructs and addresses the reader directly as "you"?

6. What does the author mean by symbols in paragraph ten? How do the examples she uses illustrate that meaning?

7. What are the final benefits of dream analysis?
8. Is the last sentence convincing?

FROM READING TO WRITING

1. Using Schmida's instructions, analyze one of your dreams. Keep a record of the stages of your analysis. Write an essay describing and evaluating the process.
2. Select a hobby or leisure activity, like rock climbing or watching movies. Using Schmida's device of addressing the reader directly, instruct the reader in the stages of this hobby or activity. Above all, work to convince the reader of the true benefits of your process.

DEFINITION

T HE WORD DEFINITION comes from the Latin word *definire*, meaning "to put an end or limit to." We are all familiar with simple definitions such as those found in the dictionary. Dictionary definitions are, in fact, useful to the essay writer. Explaining the exact meaning of a term can be a good starting point for a discussion of some aspect of the concept it represents. For instance, Karen Kowalski begins her essay "Violence in the Media" with a dictionary definition of *violence*. By defining the word violence in her introduction, she establishes common ground with her reader at the very beginning of her essay.

Unlike a simple definition, which is usually confined to one paragraph, an extended definition can make up an entire essay. For example, an extended definition of *referee* might include a history of how rules and their enforcement developed in different sports, examples and illustrations of the duties of a sports referee, and an overview of recent developments in officiating.

The use of extended definition is not confined to the expository essay. Definitions can also be used in essays that are personal and persuasive. As we saw with the use of examples, good writers usually combine different rhetorical devices to give support to their theses and maintain the interest of the reader.

Neil Bissoondath

Neil Bissoondath is a Trinidad-born Canadian writer whose works include Digging Up the Mountains *(1985),* A Casual Brutality *(1988), and* On the Eve of Uncertain Tomorrows *(1990).*

"I'm Not Racist But …"

S OMEONE RECENTLY SAID that racism is as Canadian as maple syrup. I   *1*
have no argument with that. History provides us with ample proof.
But, for proper perspective, let us remember that it is also as
American as apple pie, as French as croissants, as Jamaican as ackee, as
Indian as aloo, as Chinese as chow mein, as … Well, there's an entire
menu to be written. This is not by way of excusing it. Murder and rape,
too, are international, multicultural, as innate to the darker side of the
human experience. But we must be careful that the inevitable rage does
not blind us to the larger context.

The word "racism" is a discomforting one: it is so vulnerable to manip-   *2*
ulation. We can, if we so wish, apply it to any incident involving people
of different colour. And therein lies the danger. During the heat of alter-
cation, we seize, as terms of abuse, on whatever is most obvious about the
other person. It is, often, a question of unfortunate convenience. A
woman, because of her sex, easily becomes a female dog or an intimate
part of her anatomy. A large person might be dubbed "a stupid ox," a
small person "a little" whatever. And so a black might become "a nigger,"
a white "a honky," an Asian "a paki," a Chinese "a chink," an Italian "a
wop," a French-Canadian "a frog."

There is nothing pleasant about these terms; they assault every decent   *3*
sensibility. Even so, I once met someone who, in a stunning surge of
naiveté, used them as simple descriptives and not as terms of racial abuse.
She was horrified to learn the truth. While this may have been an extreme
case, the point is that the use of such patently abusive words may not always
indicate racial or cultural distaste. They may indicate ignorance or stupid-
ity or insensitivity, but pure racial hatred — such as the Nazis held for Jews,
or the Ku Klux Klan for blacks — is a thankfully rare commodity.

Ignorance, not the willful kind but that which comes from lack of   *4*
experience, is often indicated by that wonderful phrase, "I'm not racist
but. …" I think of the mover, a friendly man, who said, "I'm not racist,

but the Chinese are the worst drivers on the road." He was convinced this was so because the shape of their eyes, as far as he could surmise, denied them peripheral vision.

5   Or the oil company executive, an equally warm and friendly man, who, looking for an apartment in Toronto, rejected buildings with East Indian tenants not because of their race — he was telling me this, after all — but because he was given to understand that cockroaches were symbols of good luck in their culture and that, when they moved into a new home, friends came by with gift-wrapped roaches.

6   Neither of these men thought of himself as racist, and I believe they were not, deep down. (The oil company executive made it clear he would not hesitate to have me as a neighbour; my East Indian descent was of no consequence to him, my horror of cockroaches was.) Yet their comments, so innocently delivered, would open them to the accusation, justifiably so if this were all one knew about them. But it is a charge which would undoubtedly be wounding to them. It is difficult to recognize one's own misconceptions.

7   True racism is based, more often than not, on willful ignorance, and an acceptance of — and comfort with — stereotype. We like to think, in this country, that our multicultural mosaic will help nudge us into a greater openness. But multiculturalism as we know it indulges in stereotype, depends on it for a dash of colour and the flash of dance. It fails to address the most basic questions people have about each other: do those men doing the Dragon Dance really all belong to secret criminal societies? Do those women dressed in saris really coddle cockroaches for luck? Do those people in dreadlocks all smoke marijuana and live on welfare? Such questions do not seem to be the concern of the government's multicultural programs, superficial and exhibitionistic as they have become.

8   So the struggle against stereotype, the basis of all racism, becomes a purely personal one. We must beware of the impressions we create. A friend of mine once commented that, from talking to West Indians, she has the impression that their one great cultural contribution to the world is in the oft-repeated boast that "We (unlike everyone else) know how to party."

9   There are dangers, too, in community response. We must be wary of the self-appointed activists who seem to pop up in the media at every given opportunity spouting the rhetoric of retribution, mining distress for personal, political and professional gain. We must be skeptical about those who depend on conflict for their sense of self, the non-whites who need to feel themselves victims of racism, the whites who need to feel themselves purveyors of it. And we must be sure that, in addressing the problem, we do not end up creating it. Does the Miss Black Canada Beauty Contest still exist. I hope not. Not only do I find beauty contests offensive, but a racially segregated one even more so. What would the public

reaction be, I wonder, if every year CTV broadcast the *Miss White Canada Beauty Pageant*? We give community-service awards only to blacks: Would we be comfortable with such awards only for whites? In Quebec, there are The Association of Black Nurses, The Association of Black Artists, The Congress of Black Jurists. Play tit for tat: The Association of White Nurses, White Artists, White Jurists: visions of apartheid. Let us be frank, racism for one is racism for others.

Finally, and perhaps most important, let us beware of abusing the   10
word itself.

READING

1. What is the danger that Bissoondath speaks of (in paragraph two) that goes with applying the word *racism* to every incident involving people of different colour?

2. Why does the author not define the "ignorance" demonstrated by the two examples of paragraphs four and five as "true racism"? Do you agree?

3. "True racism," as he defines it, "is based, more often than not, on willful ignorance, and an acceptance of — and comfort with — stereotype." What is a stereotype? Does he propose other ways that we can think about race?

4. What is his criticism of "the government's multicultural programs"?

5. Why does he argue that the struggle against stereotype and racism is a purely personal one?

6. How does he use repetition effectively in paragraph nine?

7. Why does Bissoondath think it so important that we not abuse the word *racism*? Do you agree?

8. How do you respond to his definition of racism? How do you think it relates to your own views and experiences of race?

FROM READING TO WRITING

1. A crucial feature of definition as a rhetorical mode is the relation between definition and example. Which comes first? Do you work from definition to example or vice versa? How do you ensure that the example proves rather than disproves the definition? Explore this relation by alternately or simultaneously noting examples of racist behaviour you have observed and possible definitions of

racism. Then write a short essay using the best possible definitions and the appropriate examples.

2. Many things are notoriously difficult to define. How would you define humour, or love, or justice, or equality? This list would likely contain most of the things we regard as important. Try to define one of these things. Define it first without examples, or define it first only through examples. Then write a short essay about your experience of definition.

Ileen Rose Heer

Ileen is a Carrier Indian. She teaches classes in the Carrier language (a member of the Athabaskan language family) and is enrolled in the Native Indian Teacher Education Program at the College of New Caledonia in Prince George, BC. She is the mother of four children (three boys and a girl) and has varied interests ranging from oil painting to hunting.

She enjoys writing poems, short stories, and essays. In the future, she hopes to teach and to continue to write fiction using Native cultural content.

I'm Stringing You Along

O F ALL THE FOODS familiar to our Native Indian culture, the inno- *1* cent dried moosemeat (but beware of its deceptive appearance!) comes to mind. As I chew laboriously on a piece of this little known staple, I wonder, what is it? and who eats it?

Perhaps these questions pose little or no interest to the Caucasian, the *2* Italian, or the Mbuti Pygmy in Africa who has never been exposed to the dubious delights of this unpretentious food. This meat was made by, and for, the hardy breed who inhabit the harsh Canadian environment.

Even the dictionaries do not contain a definition of this word. The *3* encyclopedia, also, throws no light on the subject. Excuse me, there is the word dried meat in the Carrier dictionary, but who uses that? The closest the books of knowledge come to dried meat is pemmican, which is really pounded *dried meat* mixed with fat and berries. However, our simple fare is nothing as fancy as that (although it once was a majestic animal running, unconcerned for its life, through our boreal forests).

But back to my first question: what is it? Let me tell you how my mother *4* makes it. First of all she takes a large chunk of moosemeat and proceeds to attack it as if the meat were still a live moose. She slices here, chops there, slices here again, until she has a large sheet of blood-dripping red meat (I often wonder how much of the blood belongs to the now defunct moose). She hacks away at several pounds of flesh, rubbing salt into each piece, until she has enough to drape over all the poles in the smokehouse.

Meanwhile, the flies are buzzing excitedly all over the meat. Houseflies, *5* hornets, horseflies, and wasps flit into position to gorge themselves on the available treat. At this stage of the drying process, the flies are probably the only creatures that find this fare appealing! Blood is dripping all over them, but they voraciously lick one another; the more ambitious winged diners are busy gouging holes into the knife-belaboured meat. By the time my mother has the smouldering fire going, these uninvited gourmets have eaten half of the limp flesh. (I think they must have buzzed all their friends and relatives to come to dinner!)

6   My mother comes out of the smokehouse, teary-eyed but happy. I am not sure if the tears were caused by the smoke alone, or if the flies' insatiable appetites had anything to do with it! The smoke, of course, was created not only to add much-needed flavour, but to keep these selfsame flies away! So it goes — Mother checks the drying process, braving the smoke and battling the flies to protect her meagre provision. By the end of the week, the meat has dried into a board-like, impenetrable substance. Yes, it looks innocent, but beware.

7   That brings us to the question: who eats it? The young and the old of the Native Indian people do. So do those who fall in between these ages. They gnaw happily at a piece of dried meat, familiar with its aroma, flavour, and texture.

8   But for the young and the unwary, it means a lot of tugging and pulling and sucking to draw out its nutritious delights. But be careful! Don't pull too hard or you may soon be sporting a toothless smile! The elderly, too, find they have to suck and pull and tug. Be careful again. Or you will soon see your dentures lying on the floor on the other side of the room!

9   As for the rest of you who are made from hardier stock, you must also be careful, or else you will find yourselves in your dentists' chairs. Why? Oh, I forgot to tell you. This dried meat is full of strings — hamstrings, tendons, and muscles. These tend to catch between your teeth. No amount of picking with a toothpick, no amount of flossing with dental floss will dislodge these tenacious tendons!

10   Innocent? Unpretentious? Oh no, not this meat. Oh yes, I must tell you something else — dried meat can create enemies. Be careful where you sit. Make certain your companion is a true friend. You see, as you push and pull on the meat to get a bite out of it, your hand and arm can suddenly break free. And your unsuspecting neighbour will take the brunt of it. *You* will see stars and hear birds twittering as darkness takes over, dried meat forgotten!

11   Who eats dried meat? None but the wise, the alert, the knowing, and the brave — usually a Native Indian!

12   My story is finished and so is this board I was busy gnawing at all the while. Got a toothpick or floss? Thanks. Want a piece? Here, have some. No strings attached!

READING

1. What strategy does Heer use to make this definition/process essay enjoyable reading? Is this an effective strategy? Why or why not?
2. Do you think "I'm Stringing You Along" is an effective title for the essay? What is the significance of the title?
3. Would you find this Indian delicacy appealing? Why or why not?
4. What hazards are there in eating this dried meat delicacy?
5. What is the topic sentence of paragraph five? Is this paragraph unified? If so, what elements make it unified?
6. Are the transitions between paragraphs smooth? If not, how would you change them?
7. Is the conclusion appropriate and effective?
8. Although this essay is essentially an extended definition, it also contains elements of the process essay. Identify those paragraphs in which the author uses the process technique.

FROM READING TO WRITING

1. Select one of your favourite meals. Jot down in your notebook rough notes on how to prepare this meal. After making an outline, write a process essay for an audience that knows how to cook but does no know how to make this particular meal.
2. Think of a food from your culture with which other cultures are unfamiliar. In your notebook, record the qualities that are particular to this food. Then write an outline and an essay that defines the food. (Remember that your audience is someone from another culture.)

Patrick Riley

Although Patrick's mother tongue is English, his first eleven years of school were completely in French. He is currently studying general sciences at Marianopolis College in Montreal. Although Patrick has many interests, including reading, writing, painting, drawing, and playing guitar, he has yet to decide on a permanent career path. The process of committing his thoughts to paper helped him to make his own "position and ... views as a bilingual person clearer" to himself.

Anyphone

1   I AM THINKING OF WRITING SOMEDAY an authoritative dictionary of popular culture. This dictionary will be a thousand pages long and will contain two words: anglophone and francophone (and maybe an afterword on allophone). I hope this magnum opus of mine will end lifelong confusion for millions.

2   The way that some people say "anglophone community" almost leads me to believe that somewhere out there, in the vastness of Quebec, there is an isolated town where all the English-speakers live together, as recluses united by linguistic solidarity against francophones and Quebec in general.

3   What is an anglophone? Someone whose mother tongue is English? I fit that bill.

4   My parents are English-speaking Americans, who came to Montreal for several reasons, one of which was precisely because Quebec was a French/bilingual province. I went to elementary and high school in French, all the while speaking English at home. My classmates were invariably surprised when they found out that French wasn't my mother tongue. In fact I sometimes meet English-speaking people who find that I have "a French accent."

5   Anybody who knows more than one language knows that there is a trick to bilingualism (or multilingualism, as the case may be), which consists of switching mind-sets to actually *think* in the language you're speaking in. I've realized this often in my own life. There are certain people I speak to in English and others in French. To switch languages while speaking to someone requires a shift in mentality that, bizarrely enough, often changes my perception of that person. When I go to the corner store, I find myself talking to the guy behind the counter in whatever language

I happen to be thinking in at the moment. The consequence of all this is that both French and English are part of me.

Which is why participating in the anglophone–francophone dichoto- 6 my (which I believe is mostly fictitious) is, for me, equivalent to dabbling in schizophrenia. When, inevitably, the question of Quebec's distinct culture arises, I tend to treat it lightly. Some conclude that I am making fun of their heartfelt opinions and grievances. Actually, I am doing nothing of the sort. The question simply seems mostly irrelevant to me. I am part of the current Quebec culture and the idea that I should side with either "francophone" or "anglophone" seems sort of silly. I think this is the case for a growing number of people.

For this population of "bilingual" Quebeckers, of which I am a part, 7 the vocabulary used to describe political and cultural forces in the province is becoming increasingly muddled. Eventually, this misunderstanding could lead to some serious mistakes. Recently, on the front page of the *Gazette*, there was a political map of the future North America, as seen by several geographers. In the accompanying article, they cautioned that their predictions were simply that: predictions. Nevertheless, they all agreed that Quebec was destined to become independent. What's more, one of them said he thought it was going to happen "over some dead bodies." That made me sick. If you begin to believe there will be bloodshed, there will most surely be some. Independence, if it ever happens, should be a change for the better, not a cause for killing. People who take things so seriously that they lose sight of their real objectives are the most dangerous. If there were, anywhere in this universe, a malignant force of any sort, I'm sure nothing would delight and amuse it more than to see formerly peaceful Canadians maiming each other for something like the right to own Labrador.

I think that the future of so-called anglophones is just about as solid or 8 as shaky as that of all Quebeckers. I find it questionable whether the division between francophone and anglophone is actually as important as two hundred burdensome years of history have made it out to be, and whether that division has anything much to do with the future. When you think about it, the English language has actually *become* a part of Quebec culture, to the point where, if all English-speaking people were to pack up and leave tomorrow, something would definitely be missing.

The truth is that "anglophone," as well as "francophone," are merely 9 grotesque labels that fail even to represent the populations they are destined for, because they have become so tainted with prejudice and blame. What's more, they don't have much relevance to any of the issues at hand today (e.g., Quebec's relationship with Canada, with the Native peoples, its attitudes toward immigrants, etc.). If anything, they serve only to confuse discussion even more.

10   Quebec does have its own culture, but I don't think either of the two language labels is of any use in defining it. And I believe that if Quebec is to arrive at any kind of equilibrium, we have to sweep out old words and old misconceptions and look at the situation from an uncluttered perspective.

READING

1. Why does Riley claim in his introductory paragraph that he wants to write a thousand page dictionary defining only two words?

2. What tone does he establish with this statement?

3. How does his definition of himself in paragraphs three to five establish his credibility?

4. Do you think the tone in paragraphs six and seven is justified? How does this tone advance his argument?

5. Do you agree with the statements in paragraph nine? What elements of the paragraph motivate you to agree or disagree?

6. Is the author defining the two terms by refusing to define them?

7. How does the last paragraph relate to the first?

8. How would we go about creating the "uncluttered perspective" mentioned in the last sentence?

FROM READING TO WRITING

1. How would you define a Canadian? Is it necessary to define what a Canadian is? Write an essay in which you explore these questions.

2. Definitions can use classification, description, or analogy. Canadian society, for example, is often defined by the analogy of a mosaic. Try to create a new analogy to define Canada. First, note as many analogies as possible, humorous or serious. Then, begin to eliminate them until you discover an analogy you can develop into an essay.

CLASSIFICATION

C LASSIFICATION IS A FAMILIAR strategy because we use it all the time in conversation. We constantly sort or classify people, ideas, or things into groups that share common characteristics. For example, we may classify our car as a luxury car, a sports car, a family car, or a compact car. Or, using another system of classification, we may classify it as a Ford, General Motors, or Honda. This sorting process helps us to identify items and allows us to communicate our meaning more clearly to others.

Most ideas and objects can be classified. To find out if you have chosen a suitable topic for a classification essay, ask yourself if the topic can be narrowed down and divided logically into groups. For example, if you chose teachers as your subject, you could narrow this down to "teachers I have had." You could then divide the teachers you have had into three groups, such as those who inspired you, those who annoyed you, and those who bored you. Your thesis statement for this topic might be "From kindergarten to college I have had three types of teachers: those who put me to sleep, those who annoyed me, and those who left a lasting impression." An effective thesis statement in a classification essay should be like this one, simple and specific.

Classification stands midway between definition and comparison. Classification often requires definition because the nature of each group must be clear for the classification system to be meaningful to the audience. For example, in a library, groups of books are identified by a common letter or letters at the beginning of the call number. To use the classification system to find books, we need to know that PR identifies books about English literature, not books with green covers or books by women under forty.

Classification involves comparison, because the writer must establish the similarity among items in a particular group and the difference between that group and other groups. For example, a tree and a stone could be classed in different groups: living things and non-living things. Another system might group them together as natural objects, in contrast to a group of artificial objects such as pantyhose and roller coasters. Except in technical writing and textbooks, classification is rarely used as the basis of an entire expository essay. More often it forms part of an essay of comparison or cause and effect.

Robertson Davies

Born in Thamesville, Ontario, in 1913, Robertson Davies is one of Canada's greatest novelists. His most acclaimed work is The Deptford Trilogy, *composed of* Fifth Business *(1970),* The Manticore *(1972), and* World of Wonders *(1975).*

A Few Kind Words for Superstition

1   IN GRAVE DISCUSSIONS of "the renaissance of the irrational" in our time, superstition does not figure largely as a serious challenge to reason or science. Parapsychology, UFO's, miracle cures, transcendental meditation and all the paths to instant enlightenment are condemned, but superstition is merely deplored. Is it because it has an unacknowledged hold on so many of us?

2   Few people will admit to being superstitious: it implies naïveté or ignorance. But I live in the middle of a large university, and I see superstition in its four manifestations, alive and flourishing among people who are indisputably rational and learned.

3   You did not know that superstition takes four forms? Theologians assure us that it does. First is what they call Vain Observances, such as not walking under a ladder, and that kind of thing. Yet I saw a deeply learned professor of anthropology, who had spilled some salt, throwing a pinch of it over his left shoulder; when I asked him why, he replied, with a wink, that it was "to hit the Devil in the eye." I did not question him further about his belief in the Devil: but I noticed that he did not smile until I asked him what he was doing.

4   The second form is Divination, or consulting oracles. Another learned professor I know, who would scorn to settle a problem by tossing a coin (which is a humble appeal to Fate to declare itself), told me quite seriously that he had resolved a matter related to university affairs by consulting the *I Ching*. And why not? There are thousands of people on this continent who appeal to the *I Ching*, and their general level of education seems to absolve them of superstition. Almost, but not quite. The *I Ching*, to the embarrassment of rationalists, often gives excellent advice.

The third form is Idolatry, and universities can show plenty of that. If 5
you have ever supervised a large examination room, you know how many
jujus, lucky coins and other bringers of luck are placed on the desks of the
candidates. Modest idolatry, but what else can you call it?

The fourth form is Improper Worship of the True God. A while ago, I 6
learned that every day, for several days, a $2.00 bill (in Canada we have
$2.00 bills, regarded by some people as unlucky) had been tucked under a
candlestick on the altar of a college chapel. Investigation revealed that an
engineering student, worried about a girl, thought that bribery of the Deity
might help. When I talked with him, he did not think he was pricing God
cheap, because he could afford no more. A reasonable argument, but perhaps God was proud that week, for the scientific oracle went against him.

Superstition seems to run, a submerged river of crude religion, below 7
the surface of human consciousness. It has done so for as long as we have
any chronicle of human behavior, and although I cannot prove it, I doubt
if it is more prevalent today than it has always been. Superstition, the theologians tell us, comes from the Latin *supersisto*, meaning to stand in terror of the Deity. Most people keep their terror within bounds, but they
cannot root it out, nor do they seem to want to do so.

The more the teaching of formal religion declines, or takes a sociolog- 8
ical form, the less God appears to great numbers of people as a God of
Love, resuming his older form of a watchful, minatory power, to be placat-
ed and cajoled. Superstition makes its appearance, apparently unbidden,
very early in life, when children fear that stepping on cracks in the side-
walk will bring ill fortune. It may persist even among the greatly learned
and devout, as in the case of Dr. Samuel Johnson, who felt it necessary to
touch posts that he passed in the street. The psychoanalysts have their
explanation, but calling a superstition a compulsion neurosis does not
banish it.

Many superstitions are so widespread and so old that they must have 9
risen from a depth of the human mind that is indifferent to race or creed.
Orthodox Jews place a charm on their doorposts; so do (or did) the
Chinese. Some peoples of Middle Europe believe that when a man sneezes,
his soul, for that moment, is absent from his body, and they hasten to bless
him, lest the soul be seized by the Devil. How did the Melanesians come
by the same idea? Superstition seems to have a link with some body of belief
that far antedates the religions we know — religions which have no place
for such comforting little ceremonies and charities.

People who like disagreeable historical comparisons recall that when
Rome was in decline, superstition proliferated wildly, and that something 10
of the same sort is happening in our Western world today. They point to
the popularity of astrology, and it is true that sober newspapers that would
scorn to deal in love philters carry astrology columns and the fashion

magazines count them among their most popular features. But when has astrology not been popular? No use saying science discredits it. When has the heart of man given a damn for science?

11   Superstition in general is linked to man's yearning to know his fate, and to have some hand in deciding it. When my mother was a child, she innocently joined her Roman Catholic friends in killing spiders on July 11, until she learned that this was done to ensure heavy rain the day following, the anniversary of the Battle of Boyne, when the Orangemen would hold their parade. I knew an Italian, a good scientist, who watched every morning before leaving his house, so that the first person he met would not be a priest or a nun, as this would certainly bring bad luck.

12   I am not one to stand aloof from the rest of humanity in this matter, for when I was university student, a gypsy woman with a child in her arms used to appear every year at examination time, and ask a shilling of anyone who touched the Luck Baby; that swarthy infant cost me four shillings altogether, and I never failed an examination. Of course, I did it merely for the joke — or so I thought then. Now, I am humbler.

READING

1. What grounds does Davies give for classifying superstition into these four particular categories?

2. What is the effect of his taking all four illustrative examples from university life?

3. This classification is also a definition. In paragraphs seven and eight, he presents a definition of superstition. Why does superstition still persist and thrive, in Davies's view?

4. How do the sentences of paragraph nine express the similarity of superstitions in different cultures?

5. Why do you think Davies concludes with personal examples?

6. To what audience do you think the author is speaking? Aside from classifying superstitions, is he trying to persuade that audience in some way? What would he have them believe?

FROM READING TO WRITING

1. Do you do little things that cannot be explained rationally? Do you touch wood? Flee from black cats? Never walk under a ladder? Do you have personal superstitions, little habits to bring you luck, help

you win the lottery, or do well on examinations? Using Davies's classification or another, organize and classify your superstitions. Write a short essay outlining these classifications with appropriate examples.

2. Choose a type of public personality — actors, actresses, rock stars, TV news anchors, athletes, etc. — and create a system of classification for them. Write a short essay outlining and illustrating your system of classification.

Catherine Figura

"The writing process is a refining process. Once you have struggled and succeeded in producing the raw material, you must painstakingly refine it until you have deleted all the unnecessary clutter. The experience must be similar to that of a diamond cutter who has the challenge of cutting away the excess without sacrificing the core of the gem," observes Catherine. Catherine admits that she is self-conscious when she writes and always feels that she complicates her thoughts as she transfers them from mind to paper.

Catherine devoted eleven years to full-time parenthood and to her family. In 1988 she returned to university, hoping to acquire a teaching degree; however, a recent diagnosis of cancer has caused her to re-evaluate her goals and again place family at the top of her priorities.

My Private Collection of Memories

1   MY MODEST COLLECTION OF MEMORIES is stored away in a pathetic looking cardboard box that belies the value of its contents. This box is secured by a discouraging layer of dust and its flaps are frayed and torn from many openings and closings. No padlock or high-tech security system is necessary to protect this box, or its treasures, from the invasion of strangers.

2   Few things are as universal and yet as individual as the keepsake box. It doesn't seem to matter how many times I open mine; I'm always guaranteed a new voyage. Beyond the mustiness, the film of dust, and the yellowed papers are the mingling images of a personal history recognizable to no one other than its owner.

3   I always resist any attempt to catalogue the contents themselves. If I tried to systematically organize my mementos into neat piles and categories, I would be forced to give precedence to one memory over another.

4   The seasons of my box defy the calendar — Christmas cards share space with those from birthdays, anniversaries, and Valentine's Day. The sentimental and the light-hearted messages combine to create their own comfortable balance. There is no pink ribbon to hold together my letters. They hide about in groups and in isolation, classified neither by sentiment

nor author, occasion nor era. There are letters of love and of friendship, letters of apology and of gratitude. I wish I had written and received more, although I am luckier than many because I have these. I even have letters that I have written, unfinished and unsent. The thought crosses my mind to slip one in an envelope and fulfil the original intention, but greed won't allow me to part with it now. These letters and notes record the growth and development of relationships just as old photos record our physical growth and maturity. Even the particular colour of ink conveys its own information. The self-conscious slant of the lettering, the precise margins of some, the haphazard flow of others all have their tale to tell. The corny sentiments of one decade give way to the intensity of another.

But this cardboard vault hoards more than elegant prose — it is the guardian of old ticket stubs, luggage tags, and dated sales receipts. Sharing a manila envelope with random thank-you notes and *Dear Abby* columns are forgotten bank statements attesting to successful and failed attempts at financial management. And, of course, there are the first couple of paycheques — a monument to total independence. (Was that really the minimum wage? That must belong to the same fragment of history claimed by the ten-cent chocolate bar wrapper! It occurs to me that notes from my life have become items for Trivial Pursuits.) 5

Old photos that never found their way into the proper picture albums have buried themselves in my treasure box. I can recall sitting on Dawna's knee so that the camera in the narrow booth could immortalize us both in black and white. I can still hear the busy noises of the Alexis Nihon Plaza and our girlish giggles as the excitement of being on our own in the Big City overwhelmed us. (What ever happened to that choker with the peace pendant? I wonder if Dawna has the third picture.) A couple of years later, I was amassing my collection of coasters and swizzle sticks in pubs from Guy to Peel. Friday nights were different then. 6

There's the diary filled with the secret code invented by Rachel and me, the same one we used to disguise the messages we exchanged in eighth-grade English class. Funny, the code seems so transparent now. If this diary were opened to a curious audience, it would spill out all the secrets of our 12-year-old hearts. (Someone once told me that Rachel had become a nun. Funny, she used to dream of becoming a jockey! I wish we had stayed in touch.) 7

There is a miniature book of love poems — commercially popular around the same time as packaged horoscopes. And the book of matches tells of habits overcome, but, more, it reflects a way that was, attitudes and values changed en masse. 8

An old, discarded address book records its own history. Those were the days when apartments were changed more frequently than hairdos, 9 and rated according to the nearest pizzeria. Every move meant a search for the best pizza, and the research was carried out with great enthusiasm.

10   Competition was tight in a city that produces the best. Every street in Little Italy had its master of perfect crust. It had to be neither too thick nor too thin, too hard nor too soft. The sauce had to be made from just certain tomatoes and the perfect combination of basil and oregano from Mama's recipe. The pepperoni had to be thrown on randomly, mushrooms had to be tossed on generously, and the cheese (by far the most important ingredient) had to be abundantly piled and melted so that it could stretch from the box across the table to your plate without even a hint of separation! Pizza was synonymous with dining, and no social occasion or Saturday night was complete without it. After class, after work, after bowling, or with a game of charades, there was always Montreal's greatest culinary feast. Of course, there was Dante's on that day; the chef burned the pizza, but we didn't care. The romance ended when the news broke about the cheese factory and the mice!

11   Times change; I can rarely eat more than one piece of pizza these days. There is a new generation already a part of my memory bank. Alongside my own fading school picture is a miniature hospital band labelled: Boy — Figura, Catherine. Congratulation cards are mixed in with those from the wedding. The inventory is a random one, as it should be. My mind and soul hold no clock, no calendar; and this cardboard box is merely an extension of those.

12   Three decades of life are too much to relive in one visit. I somehow never make it to the bottom half of the box. It is all the more intriguing for its untravelled reflection. The abundance of personal history has given rise to a second box. *Dear Abby* has been replaced by Lynn Johnston's *For Better or For Worse*. As I hoard away little pieces of other people in my attempt to save some of what we have shared, I wonder if, by chance, there is a letter, signed with my love, in someone else's cardboard box.

READING

1. What rhetorical modes, other than classification, does Figura use in her essay? Cite an example of each.

2. What is the tone of her essay?

3. How many years of memories are represented in her collection? From what age to what age is covered? Explain your answer.

4. How does the author convey the period of her life to which a particular memory belongs? Give examples.

5. What might she mean in paragraph six when she writes "Friday nights were different then"?

6. The concluding paragraph of an essay usually serves to round out the subject. Often it echoes the introduction. Does the conclusion of this essay follow this guideline? Why or why not?

FROM READING TO WRITING

1. Is there a picture, card, piece of jewellery, or other object that elicits a particular response every time you pick it up and look at it? Try to remember everything you can about the day this object came into your possession, who gave it to you, what meaning it has for you. Write an essay describing the significance of the object. Be sure to provide enough background details to let your reader understand the object's importance to you.

2. One of the most popular pastimes is collecting. People collect a vast range of objects: stamps, antiques, rocks, comic books, even bottle caps. Write an essay that attempts to explain why people collect things.

Laura J. Turner

Laura returned to school after "ten or so enjoyable and successful years in public relations" and is currently an English major at the University of Regina. Laura says she has a "fascination with the language; words have a curious power within the sentence," and that if you "look after the words, their sound, meaning, flow, cadence, and connotation ... the sentences look after themselves. This is also true of sentences and paragraphs." Although Laura finds the writing process "to be always long and arduous," she says that "after extensive revision, when the product finally looks and feels right, I am rewarded with a gratifying feeling of accomplishment."

Truth or Consequences

1   WHEN WE INTENTIONALLY make false statements, we lie. Lies are regarded as sins, vices, transgressions, and immoral offences. Lies are not modern phenomena: lies have been around forever. They permeate all cultures and all eras of history; lies are universal. That we should not lie is implied by one of the Ten Commandments. Nevertheless, whether we are pious or not, we generally agree that lies are socially and morally wrong. We despise lies, and more especially, we despise liars. We regard liars as social deviants, reprobates; we rank them near the bottom of the social hierarchy. Still, we all lie.

2   We are inherently prone to lying, I suppose because we are subject to original sin. To tell a lie is to be intrinsically human. Yet we regard lying as wicked depravity while, at the same time, we continue to lie. Lies come in different shapes and sizes. Though all are lies by definition, some lies are sanctioned by society, some are tolerated and others, of course, frowned upon. How are we able simultaneously to hold these conflicting viewpoints concerning lies? We classify lies as little white lies, half-truths, and barefaced lies and then impose upon them a ranking according to their degree of social acceptance or the severity of their immorality.

3   We categorize lies so that little white lies are less profane and more socially and morally acceptable than the lies of the opposite end of the scale, barefaced lies; half-truths fall in the middle range. In other words, this hierarchical system of lies we have developed enables us to justify the

telling of harmless little white lies, to condone half-truths, and to disapprove of barefaced lies.

We first encounter little white lies at birth; we are cooed at: "My, isn't 4 she beautiful. She looks just like you." This is a lie, albeit a little white lie. Babies are not beautiful; they are red and wrinkly and do not resemble their parents at all. Little white lies are often told by kind, polite persons in an attempt to be socially or politically correct. When we wish to say the right thing, spare someone's feelings, pay a compliment, or make someone feel better, we make selfless statements that bend or stretch the truth, usually to benefit someone else.

If we tell little white lies to be courteous, then we tell half-truths often 5 to benefit or protect ourselves. We neglect to tell the whole truth, opting instead to omit the incriminating half of the story. Other half-truths are merely exaggerations. Many half-truths, like little white lies, are part of ordinary, daily conversation. Half-truths seem less brash and, perhaps, more socially and morally forgivable, but the omitted half can haunt. Yet half-truths have become so hackneyed that many exist as clichés in our society. "I gave at the office," "the cheque is in the mail," "we'll do lunch," and "I'll call you sometime" are everyday jargon; they illustrate the social amnesty granted the telling of half-truths.

Barefaced lies are socially unacceptable. Liars of the barefaced genre 6 are self-centred and self-serving. Barefaced lies are committed in the pursuit of profit, prestige, power, vengeance, or any combination of these moral turpitudes. The barefaced liar has little or no concern for the welfare of others. A barefaced liar might be the accused in a murder trial who, without conscience, declares himself "not guilty" when, in fact, he has killed someone. A barefaced liar may be someone who emphatically declares "I *am* telling you the truth!" or "no, I definitely didn't do that!" — claiming innocence, or denying guilt, when the opposite is true. A moral felon who falls into this area of the lie labyrinth lies consciously and deliberately. Thus, the barefaced lie of the pathological liar is regarded as the most iniquitous of lies.

Regardless of which category one may have lied his or her way into, it 7 is not the committing of the lie, but the lie's potential to cause hurt or damage, that becomes the measure of its sinfulness. Because the majority of lies fall in the little white lie and half-truth categories, and so are less severe than barefaced lies, lying has become commonplace. One of the qualities that distinguishes humans from other creatures is our ability to justify and rationalize our behaviour, especially our deviant behaviour. Toward this end, we have ranked and classified lies so that some, such as little white lies, and half-truths, are tolerable while barefaced lies are regarded as offences. We are more able to accept white lies and half-truths because we can rationalize that the ends justify the means.

READING

1. How does Turner use the first sentence of the essay? What is the relation of this sentence to the first paragraph?
2. What is the effect of the short sentence at the end of the first paragraph?
3. How does the author use the last sentence of the second paragraph? What is the relation of this sentence to that paragraph and to the essay as a whole?
4. How does the classification in the first paragraph lead to the classification in the second?
5. How does Turner make the transition in paragraph three from the final three-part classification to the rest of the essay?
6. How do paragraphs four to six develop and illustrate the basis of the classification?
7. Do you think that the author's system of classification covers all forms of lies?
8. Do you agree with the conclusions made in the last paragraph?

FROM READING TO WRITING

1. Think of other forms of behaviour generally understood as virtues or vices, like charity or love, cheating or stealing. Note all the varieties of this behaviour you can identify. Then discover a basis for classification, a way to define, distinguish, and organize these varieties. Then write an essay developing this classification.

COMPARISON AND CONTRAST

A COMPARISON ESTABLISHES how two or more objects or ideas resemble each other and how they differ. Comparison is a vital tool of exposition because it forces us to look at our subjects in a detailed, systematic way. When you compare, say, an apple and an orange, you first establish a number of criteria relevant to your purpose. If you simply want your reader to be able to identify these fruits and not confuse them, you will choose sensory criteria such as size, shape, colour, skin, and texture. If you are discussing apples and oranges as agricultural crops, you might choose climate, growing season, methods of harvesting, commercial value, diseases, and pests.

There are two ways to organize a comparison and contrast essay. The first way, known as the block (or chunk) method, involves dividing the essay into two major blocks or chunks. The first block discusses one of the subjects of the comparison; the second block discusses the other subject. George Duff uses this method to organize his essay "Co-operative Games." Here is an outline of his essay:

Paragraph one	Introduction
Paragraph two	The game *Civilization*
	1. Purpose: development of culture
	2. Development depends upon co-operation, not conflict
Paragraph three	The game *Republic of Rome*
	1. Purpose: political advancement
	2. Advancement depends on co-operation and greatest success for all
Paragraph four	Conclusion

The block method works best for short, simple essays, like Duff's, that involve only a few points of comparison.

The second way to organize a comparison and contrast essay is the point-by-point (or slice) method. This method involves dividing the essay into several main points and comparing the two subjects under each point. Karen Kowalski uses this method in her essay "Violence in the Media." Here is an outline of Karen's essay:

Paragraph one	Introduction
Paragraph two	Violence against women
	—*Dead Ringers*
	—*Road Warrior*
Paragraph three	Violent situations

	—*Dead Ringers*
	—*Road Warrior*
Paragraph four	Psychological and physical aspects of
	violence
	—*Dead Ringers*
	—*Road Warrior*
Paragraph five	Conclusion

The point-by-point method works best for longer, more complex comparison and contrast essays because it allows the reader to focus on the complexity of the comparison being made.

Although writers may use comparison and contrast as one of several rhetorical devices within one essay, comparison and contrast is often used as an organizing principle for an entire essay. Whether you use the block method or the point-by-point method, the technique should convey to your readers fundamental similarities and significant differences.

George Duff

George is a full-time undergraduate at the University of Toronto specializing in Peace and Conflict studies. While writing this piece, George discovered that "it is much easier to communicate something which is understood well," and that for him, the structure, "which allows for development of detail as required, once the logical arrangement is sound," comes first.

Co-operative Games

THE CURRENT TREND in adult board games is toward games involving   1
more than two players and emphasizing co-operation rather than
conflict. Two excellent examples are the *Civilization* and *Republic of Rome* games published by Avalon Hill. In these games, the players are motivated by the mechanics of play to enter into co-operative relationships while maintaining the excitement of competition. The players compete in parallel, making gains toward their goals that do not directly cause the other players any loss. On the surface, these games are similar, both of them set in the ancient world of history, but they are representatives of two different methods in the design of co-operative games. *Civilization* requires a strategic approach, while *Republic* has political dynamics.

Civilization places each player in control of a developing culture in the   2
ancient Mediterranean world. Their populations are represented by tokens on the mapboard, and the progress of each culture from Stone Age to Iron Age is marked on a track to the side. As the game goes on, these populations grow larger, build cities, and enter into trade with each other. In order to advance, a player must achieve cultural gains such as "Agriculture" or "Law"; failure to do so will hold that player back. The first to pass through all of the requirements wins. The players do not compete directly because the game mechanics are such that conflicts will harm both aggressor and victim; successful play involves negotiation and trade agreements rather than warfare and conflict. Generally, the player who is fair in trade will win out over one who attempts to defeat and conquer his neighbours as he might in a game of chess.

In *Republic*, the players assume the roles of influential senators in a   3
period of early Roman history. The game involves a sophisticated system that simulates the democratic structure of the Roman government of the

time. Together, the players must react to events such as foreign wars, epidemics, and riots; if the affairs of state are handled poorly, *all* the players lose and the game is over. Within the constraints established by this threat, the players compete for status, popularity, and wealth; if one of a player's senators achieves sufficient influence, he is declared the winner. Under these conditions, the players must seek to maximize their personal gains without becoming too greedy, shifting from alliance to opposition and from faction to faction as prudence dictates. The competition between players overlaps with their dependence upon one another; trickery and bargaining are useful talents for a player. Threat is also an element, as the assassination of an opposing senator is an option of last resort available to all players.

4   The difference between the two games lies in the motive for co-operation. *Civilization* induces co-operation by promoting trade as the most effective method for achieving goals. *Republic* achieves co-operation by forcing the players to come to some sort of agreement under the threat of universal failure. Also, in the *Civilization* game, the players identify with a unique structure that exists independently. Although they interfere with one another, each is free to make an analysis and to pursue strategy. The *Republic* game places the players in a situation where their mutual interest can suffer through the irresponsibility of any single individual. Hence they must temper self-interest with a wider concern for the group. In this game, strategy is supplanted by politics as the players move through a spectrum of attitudes from pure co-operation to ruthless ambition.

READING

1. To compare and contrast two things is to put them side by side, or to make them parallel. How does Duff use parallels in his introductory paragraph?

2. How does he explore and develop these parallels between the games in the second and third paragraphs?

3. Parallelism is also a stylistic device in which similar ideas are compared and contrasted in similar sentence structures. What examples of parallelism do you see in the third paragraph?

4. To compare and to contrast is to discover similarities and differences. How are the rules of the two games, as the author presents them, similar and different?

5. What values do these rules reflect?

6. What conclusions does Duff invite us to make about these values?

7. What is the significance of the subject matter of the two games — the history of Mediterranean civilization and of the early Roman republic — for these conclusions?

8. How does the concluding paragraph reflect and develop the parallels of the introductory paragraph and the parallels between the second and third paragraphs?

FROM READING TO WRITING

1. Write an essay in which you compare and contrast two games of the same type, for example, baseball and hockey, or bridge and poker. Begin by discovering the parallels between the rules of the two games. Reflect on the significance of these similarities and differences. What values do these two games embody? What do they demonstrate about those who play them?

2. Select any other two examples of any type of recreation or entertainment — two movies, two television shows, two musical groups, etc. — that you find especially significant. Write an essay exploring and developing the parallels between them.

Karen Kowalski

Karen is currently enrolled in the Education program at the University of Calgary. Outside of classes, Karen devotes much of her time to volunteering at the Alberta Children's Hospital or working with the learning disabled and the handicapped. Upon graduation, she hopes either to teach Grade 3 or to continue on to a Master's degree in Child Psychology.

During the process of writing "Violence in the Media," Karen learned that "ideas and sentences flow easily if you don't pressure yourself into thinking too hard about the topic. Once you have a general idea, let the details flow and write whatever comes into your head until you exhaust all possibilities. Then, form the ideas into a coherent, significant whole."

Violence in the Media

1   THE MERRIAM-WEBSTER DICTIONARY defines violence as:

1: exertion of physical force so as to injure 2: injury by or as if by infringement or profanation 3: intense or furious and often destructive action or force 4: vehement feeling or expression: INTENSITY.

2   We are exposed to violence through the media every day. The effects of this exposure on society are largely dependent on the way in which violence is represented. Violence may be conveyed through the media several different ways. It may be implicitly or explicitly rendered in a realistic or fantastic setting, and may operate on a physical or psychological level. Two movies that differ in their representation of violence are *Dead Ringers* and *Road Warrior*. While the violence in the former is implicit, realistic, and psychological, the violence in the latter is explicit, fantastic, and phical. Although the violence of both *Dead Ringers* and *Road Warriors* is disturbing, the representation of violence in *Dead Ringers* as implicit, realistic, and psychological is more harmful in its effects than the representation of violence in *Road Warrior*.

3   The way in which the violence differs in the two movies becomes evident when contrasting the portrayal of violence against women. The violence against women in *Dead Ringers* is continuous throughout the movie but it is always an implied violence. The audience is never actually witness to the details of a violent act being performed. The camera is angled

in such a way that the viewer rarely catches a glimpse of blood. The impact of the violence in this movie is achieved by focussing on both the sounds and the facial expressions of the gynecological patients, and by giving the audience the opportunity to exercise their imaginations. In *Road Warrior*, on the other hand, violence against women is portrayed in only one scene, but the scene is very strong and extremely explicit. In this case, the audience is exposed visually to every cruel detail of a gang rape. The camera is directed toward the action so that the audience is able to view the entire scene. The impact of violence in this movie is achieved by fast, brutal, visual detail; it leaves nothing to the imagination. Imagination plays a key role in the effects of violence. When members of the audience use their minds to achieve an image, that image is more likely to stay with them in the long run.

Another way to explain why the violence in *Dead Ringers* has more of   4 an impact than the violence in *Road Warrior* is to contrast the situations of both movies. The situation in *Dead Ringers* is realistic. The events of the movie occur in the present, in a city that is familiar to the audience, and revolve around a very real part of many people's lives — a doctor's office. The violence in this movie is especially affecting for women because almost every civilized woman, at least once in her life, has to face the stirrups during a gynecological examination. As a society we look up to and trust doctors with our lives. To view doctors abusing patients can make for a very disturbing form of violence. The situation in *Road Warrior* is very different in that it is fantastic. The events of this movie occur in the future after nuclear holocaust, in a place that is unfamiliar, and the events centre around the search for gasoline — a search that the general population has not yet been faced with. The fantasy of the movie is portrayed through the setting and the fact that the two groups going to war resemble hard core punk rockers. Because *Road Warrior* is fantasy, the audience may more readily separate their everyday lives from the incidents that occur within the context of the movie. Because the focus of the situation of *Dead Ringers* is realistic and does not allow for easy separation from everyday life, the violence of the movie will have more of an impact on the audience.

A third and final way to explain why the violence in *Dead Ringers* has   5 more impact on an audience than the violence in *Road Warrior* is to contrast the psychological and physical aspects of the movies. *Dead Ringers* is violent in a more psychological than physical way. The violence in the movie results from the demented minds of the two doctors. Their abuse of women, their abuse of drugs, and their subsequent abuse of their practice are brought on by their obsessive relationship with one another. The doctors are identical twins who live in constant fear of losing each other. Although their personalities may appear different on the surface, they really are very much alike. The twins feel the same way, love the same women, and fear the same things. It is their psychological difficulties that tie the audience into the movie. In *Road Warrior*, on the other hand, the violence is purely physical. It is a typical "rack 'em up and hack 'em up" movie. War is the motivation for the violence in this movie and the motivation for the war is the quest to attain all the gasoline remaining in the land. The violence in this movie occurs through bloodshed, decapitation, and dismemberment. The audience is better able to relate to the psychological violence in *Dead Ringers* than to the physical violence in *Road Warrior* because we have more of an ability to feel psychological violence than physical violence.

6   The effects that violence in the media have on an audience are dependent on the way in which violence is represented. Violence represented in an implicit, realistic, and psychological manner, as in *Dead Ringers*, has a more harmful effect on an audience than violence represented in an explicit, fantastic, and physical manner, as in *Road Warrior*. When the members of an audience are given the opportunity to exercise their imaginations and to experience the violence in a realistic setting they can relate to, the violence in the movie will have a greater impact on them.

READING

1. Who is Kowalski's audience? Cite specific examples from her essay in your answer.

2. What is her thesis? Do you think she proves her thesis? Why or why not?

3. What are the various types of violence that the author describes? What type does she attribute to each of the films she considers?

4. Do you think that the first paragraph is an effective introduction to the essay? Why or why not?

5. Does Kowalski make effective use of the transitions within and between paragraphs? Cite three examples of transitions from her essay.

6. Would the reader understand her explanation without having seen the films being discussed? Why or why not?

7. Does the final paragraph effectively summarize the thesis?

8. "Violence in the Media" contains elements of the persuasive essay. Has the author used logic effectively in her essay? Why or why not?

FROM READING TO WRITING

1. Saturday morning children's television has been cited as one of the causes of violent behaviour in children and in adults who grew up with violent cartoons. Watch a morning of cartoons and record the details of at least three violent incidents. Then write a persuasive essay in which you argue either that violence in children's cartoons should be banned or that children's cartoons should be allowed to continue as they are. (Your audience is someone who holds the opposite opinion.)

2. Statistics show that the incidence of violent crime in Canadian society is increasing. What do you think causes violence in a society? Organize your thoughts in your notebook before writing a cause and effect essay on this subject. (Your audience comprises concerned citizens who would like to find ways to eliminate crime.)

Anna Quindlen

Anna Quindlen is a regular columnist for The New York Times. She has collected the best of her columns in Living Out Loud (1988). In the following essay, first published in 1988, she compares her sons Quin and Christopher.

The Knight and the Jester

1   SOMETIMES I THINK you can tell everything about my two children by watching them sleep at night. One lies flat on his back, the quilt tucked neatly under his armpits, his arms at his side, as though he were a child miming perfect sleep for an advertisement for cocoa or pajamas. No matter what time it is, you will find him so.

2   The other will be sprawled in some corner of the bed, and on the floor will be his quilt, his sheets, his pillow and, if he's feeling particularly froggy, his pajamas. Sometimes he is at the head and sometimes he is at the foot, and sometimes half of him is hanging over the side. For the sake of futile mothering gestures, I will often cover him up, but if I return 15 minutes later the quilt will be on the floor again. I look from one bed to the other and think: the knight and the jester; the gentleman and the wild man; the parson and the gambler.

3   I like to think there are no particular value judgments to these assessments, but that is not true. I try to suppress them sometimes, to think in terms of body temperature as I straighten one set of perfectly straight blankets and untangle another from the floor. It is not fair to make two children foils for one another, although it is common and, I suppose, understandable to do so. It can also turn to poison faster than you can say Cain and Abel, for sometimes the unconscious assessments become sharper: the good child and the bad one; the smart one and the stupid one; the success and the failure. And sometimes thinking makes it so.

4   Perhaps I am overly sensitive on this subject, since I grew up with its shadow. I have a brother barely a year younger than I am, and I suspect that both of us were thoroughly sick, after a while, of the comparisons. Deep down we were not so different, but it was inevitable that in finding his own way around the world, one of the things he wanted was to find a way that was different from mine. By high school, I had become the circle-pin princess of the junior class. My brother, meanwhile, had begun to

affect black leather jackets and shoes with pointed toes. If we had had a buck for every teacher who was incredulous that we shared the same parents, we could have started a small business together.

It was not as bad for me as it was for him, since I got the prime position at the starting gate, and he got the "on the other hand." Sometimes I think it turned him into some things he wasn't, just for the sake of living out the contrast.

Now I know how easily it happens, as we play out our liking for prototypes here, in the little bedrooms and the playgrounds and at the kitchen table. At some point after the first child is born, we ditch the books and learn the lessons of eating, sleeping and talking by doing. And in the process what we come to know about children is what the first child teaches us. We use that to measure the progress of the next child. And quietly, subtly, without malice or bad intentions, begins the process of comparison.

Some say that this is in the nature of being second, and that the person a second child becomes has more to do with filling in the spaces that haven't been claimed yet than with some innate difference of temperament. It's easy sometimes for me to believe that. My children are quite different. The eldest had staked out early the territory of being sensitive, sweet, thoughtful and eager to please. There were openings in the areas of independence, confidence, creative craziness and pure moxie, and whether by coincidence or design, the second child has all those things.

Yet when I think of the theory of filling in the family blanks I think, too, of two babies in utero, one slow and languorous and giving no trouble, the other a real pistol, pounding the pavement, dancing the fandango, throwing his sheets on the floor even while floating in amniotic fluid. And I remember that in every knight there is something of the jester; in every wild man, a bit of the gentleman. The danger in making our children take roles on opposite sides of the family room is that the contradictions in their own characters, the things that make humans so interesting, get flattened out and hidden away. The other danger is that they will hate one another.

So far, I think we are doing all right. Certainly there's little hatred, for which I am deeply grateful. But in my attempts to make our chaotic lives orderly, I have to battle constantly against the urge to pigeonhole each of them, to file away the essentials of their personalities as one thing I've finally gotten down, once and for all. I have never said to either, "Why can't you be more like your brother?" I have never compared them aloud. I am always mindful of my mother's will, in which she noted that I was everything she was not; this happened to be true, but since at the time I though everything she was was wonderful, it left me little doubt about my own inadequacies.

10   And in truth one boy is not everything the other is not. Both of them are everything — obedient, willful, sensitive, tough, wild, pacific — in different measures. Both look like angels when they are asleep, although neither is anything quite so two-dimensional as angelic. Children are not easy, no matter what mothers sometimes like to think in their attempts to turn all this tortured family calculus into plain arithmetic.

READING

1. How do the words and sentences of Quindlen's first two paragraphs compare and contrast her sons?

2. Why does the author try "to think in terms of body temperature" in paragraph three?

3. What is the effect of her mentioning Cain and Abel in the third paragraph?

4. How would you describe the process of thinking that she is trying to analyze in herself?

5. What does she mean when she writes that "we play out our liking for prototypes" in the process of comparison?

6. How does the process of comparison work as she outlines it? Can you think of other examples of this process at work?

7. How do the sentences in paragraph eight express the process of comparison?

8. How does Quindlen attempt to balance, if not resolve, the difficulties created by comparison?

9. Do you agree with Quindlen that comparisons are inevitable?

FROM READING TO WRITING

1. Select two of anything. Begin by noting all the similarities and differences between the two things. Then begin to develop the structure of an essay by letting the similarities and differences arrange themselves into groups or categories. Write a short essay outlining and developing these categories. Throughout, try to use the features of style — words, sentences, paragraphs, figures, etc. — that express the process of comparison.

ANALOGY

OMPARISON AND CONTRAST were used to point out similarities and differences between two like things in the essays in the last section. On the other hand, an analogy is used to compare two very different things to demonstrate a point. In the chapter on description in Part 2 we discussed the simile, which uses *like* or *as* (his voice was like the wind in winter) and the metaphor, which does not (his roaring was a wind in winter). Both these figures of speech are used primarily to give a vivid impression of the qualities of the thing being described.

In its broader meaning, any simile is a type of analogy. However, the classic analogy compares not qualities but relations ("Knowledge is to the mind what light is to the eye") and is used primarily to make a point clear or to support an argument. In logic, an analogy is the inference that things similar in one respect will probably be similar in another respect. We used an analogy in Part 1 when we compared revising an essay to glass blowing. First we established a basic similarity between the two processes: manipulating words or blowing glass to produce something that is both functional and attractive. Then we drew a further comparison between the handling of a flawed glass plate and a flawed essay: just as the plate is broken up and remade until it is right, so should the essay be revised until it is right.

Analogies can make a discussion of abstract issues more graphic and lively; they sometimes help the reader understand a point that would be difficult to grasp directly. ("Imagine that the universe is a piece of paper and the planets are points drawn upon it. If you fold the piece of paper, there will be a shorter distance between two points than the distance along the paper. Just so, multidimensional theories predict that space can be folded, bringing together points far apart in space.")

Sometimes, entire essays can be constructed around an analogy. In this chapter, Clint Saulteaux draws an analogy between the history of the buffalo and the aboriginal people of Canada. The analogy allows him to discover the similarities in differences and cause for hope in difficulty. The analogy allows him an expression of powerful emotions through rich and evocative language.

In "Lunchroom Wars," Nan Laurenzio does not draw a formal analogy, but her extended metaphor of a battle implies analogies between children at lunch and armies at war.

> ... the opposing cavalry was positioned close enough to the attackers' post that salami, flung at close range, had a superb slapping impact on the target. Ducking just in time, I was witness to the morbid mutilation of a brightly

coloured Dole orange bomb as it crashed against the grey barrier and splattered to its soggy death. The hostilities continued and no sooner had a badly bruised banana, oozing from its torn peel, been bombarded in return, than the prized half-full container of Laura Secord's vanilla pudding was hurled back as the final blow. The opponents, temporarily out of ammunition, resorted to war cries that reverberated from the walls, floor, and ceiling and were shot with enough resonance to resemble the Concorde flying low overhead.

While an analogy occasionally forms the basis of an entire essay, as we have seen from the above examples, more often we use an analogy to illustrate one point in an essay. For example, Marty J. Chan begins his essay "Fall from University Grace" with a partial analogy. Good writers are always observing and analyzing human behaviour, looking for new ways to express ideas more vividly to their readers.

Annie Dillard

Annie Dillard recently published her first novel, The Living *(1992).
The following essay is from her much celebrated collection* Pilgrim at
Tinker Creek *(1974), an account of her life at Tinker Creek in the
Roanoke Valley in Virginia.*

Untying the Knot

YESTERDAY I SET OUT TO CATCH the new season, and instead I 1
found an old snakeskin. I was in the sunny February woods by the
quarry; the snakeskin was lying in a heap of leaves right next to
an aquarium someone had thrown away. I don't know why that someone
hauled the aquarium deep into the woods to get rid of it; it had only one
broken glass side. The snake found it handy, I imagine; snakes like to rub
against something rigid to help them out of their skins, and the broken
aquarium looked like the nearest likely object. Together the snakeskin
and the aquarium made an interesting scene on the forest floor. It looked
like an exhibit at a trial — circumstantial evidence — of a wild scene, as
though a snake had burst through the broken side of the aquarium, burst
through his ugly old skin, and disappeared, perhaps straight up in the air,
in a rush of freedom and beauty.

The snakeskin had unkeeled scales, so it belonged to a nonpoisonous 2
snake. It was roughly five feet long by the yardstick, but I'm not sure
because it was very wrinkled and dry, and every time I tried to stretch it
flat it broke. I ended up with seven or eight pieces of it all over the
kitchen table in a fine film of forest dust.

The point I want to make about the snakeskin is that when I found it, 3
it was whole and tied in a knot. Now there have been stories told, even by
reputable scientists, of snakes that have deliberately tied themselves in a
knot to prevent larger snakes from trying to swallow them — but I
couldn't imagine any way that throwing itself into a half hitch would help
a snake trying to escape its skin. Still, ever cautious, I figured that one of
the neighborhood boys could possibly have tied it in a knot in the fall, for
some whimsical boyish reason, and left it there, where it dried and gath-
ered dust. So I carried the skin along thoughtlessly as I walked, snagging it
sure enough on a low branch and ripping it in two for the first of many
times. I saw that thick ice still lay on the quarry pond and that the skunk

cabbage was already out in the clearings, and then I came home and looked at the skin and its knot.

4   The knot had no beginning. Idly I turned it around in my hand, searching for a place to untie; I came to with a start when I realized I must have turned the thing around fully ten times. Intently, then, I traced the knot's lump around with a finger: it was continuous. I couldn't untie it any more than I could untie a doughnut; it was a loop without beginning or end. These snakes are magic, I thought for a second, and then of course I reasoned what must have happened. The skin had been pulled inside-out like a peeled sock for several inches; then an inch or so of the inside-out part — a piece whose length was coincidentally equal to the diameter of the skin — had somehow been turned right-side out again, making a thick lump whose edges were lost in wrinkles, looking exactly like a knot.

5   So. I have been thinking about the change of seasons. I don't want to miss spring this year. I want to distinguish the last winter frost from the out-of-season one, the frost of spring. I want to be there on the spot the moment the grass turns green. I always miss this radical revolution; I see it the next day from a window, the yard so suddenly green and lush I could envy Nebuchadnezzar down on all fours eating grass. This year I want to stick a net into time and say "now," as men plant flags on the ice and snow and say, "here." But it occurred to me that I could no more catch spring by the tip of the tail than I could untie the apparent knot in the snakeskin; there are no edges to grasp. Both are continuous loops.

6   I wonder how long it would take you to notice the regular recurrence of the seasons if you were the first man on earth. What would it be like to live in open-ended time broken only by days and nights? You could say, "it's cold again; it was cold before," but you couldn't make the key connection and say, "it was cold this time last year," because the notion of "year" is precisely the one you lack. Assuming that you hadn't noticed an orderly progression of heavenly bodies, how long would you have to live on earth before you could feel with any assurance that any one particular long period of cold would, in fact, end? "While the earth remaineth, seedtime and harvest, and cold and heat, and summer and winter, and day and night shall not cease": God makes this guarantee very early in Genesis to a people whose fears on this point had perhaps not been completely allayed.

7   It must have been fantastically important, at the real beginnings of human culture, to conserve and relay this vital seasonal information, so that the people could anticipate dry or cold seasons, and not huddle on some November rock hoping pathetically that spring was just around the corner. We still very much stress the simple fact of four seasons to school children; even the most modern of modern new teachers, who don't seem to care if their charges can read or write or name two products of Peru,

will still muster some seasonal chitchat and set the kids to making paper pumpkins, or tulips, for the walls. "The people," wrote Van Gogh in a letter, "are very sensitive to the changing seasons." That we are "very sensitive to the changing seasons" is, incidentally, one of the few good reasons to shun travel. If I stay at home I preserve the illusion that what is happening on Tinker Creek is the very newest thing, that I'm at the very vanguard and cutting edge of each new season. I don't want the same season twice in a row; I don't want to know I'm getting last week's weather, used weather, weather broadcast up and down the coast, old-hat weather.

But there's always unseasonable weather. What we think of the 8 weather and behavior of life on the planet at any given season is really all a matter of statistical probabilities; at any given point, anything might happen. There is a bit of every season in each season. Green plants — deciduous green leaves — grow everywhere, all winter long, and small shoots come up pale and new in every season. Leaves die on the tree in May, turn brown, and fall into the creek. The calendar, the weather, and the behavior of wild creatures have the slimmest of connections. Everything overlaps smoothly for only a few weeks each season, and then it all tangles up again. The temperature, of course, lags far behind the calendar seasons, since the earth absorbs and releases heat slowly, like a leviathan breathing. Migrating birds head south in what appears to be dire panic, leaving mild weather and fields full of insects and seeds; they reappear as if in all eagerness in January, and poke about morosely in the snow. Several years ago our October woods would have made a dismal colored photograph for a sadist's calendar: a killing frost came before the leaves had even begun to brown; they dropped from every tree like crepe, blackened and limp. It's all a chancy, jumbled affair at best, as things seem to be below the stars.

Time is the continuous loop, the snakeskin with scales endlessly over- 9 lapping without beginning or end, or time is an ascending spiral if you will, like a child's toy Slinky. Of course we have no idea which arc on the loop is our time, let alone where the loop itself is, so to speak, or down whose lofty flight of stairs the Slinky so uncannily walks.

The power we seek, too, seems to be a continuous loop. I have always 10 been sympathetic with the early notion of a divine power that exists in a particular place, or that travels about over the face of the earth as a man might wander — and when he is "there" he is surely not here. You can shake the hand of a man you meet in the woods; but the spirit seems to roll along like the mythical hoop snake with its tail in its mouth. There are no hands to shake or edges to untie. It rolls along the mountain ridges like a fireball, shooting off a spray of sparks at random, and will not be trapped, slowed, grasped, fetched, peeled, or aimed. "As for the wheels, it was cried unto them in my hearing, O wheel." This is the hoop of flame that shoots the rapids in the creek or spins across the dizzy meadows; this is the arsonist of the sunny woods: catch it if you can.

READING

1. An opening paragraph should introduce the topic by providing ideas or images that will be developed in the essay. What ideas or images does Dillard use in her introduction?
2. What "edges" is the author so concerned to catch?
3. Why do you think she wants to distinguish the last winter frost from the first spring one? How could this be done?
4. One paragraph should develop logically and naturally from the next. How does paragraph seven develop out of paragraph six?
5. What is the central analogy of this essay? Does Dillard show other, secondary analogies?
6. Why do you think she uses analogy? Why does analogy especially suit what she wants to express?
7. How does the last paragraph connect with the first. Does this connection express in some way the idea of "the mythical hoop snake with its tail in its mouth"?

FROM READING TO WRITING

1. Think of analogies from your own experience for the change of seasons or the passage of time. Think of serious analogies and humorous ones like Dillard's Slinky toy. Select one central analogy and write a short essay developing it and incorporating as many others as are appropriate.
2. In an analogy, the two things compared must be different and similar. Usually, one is an abstract or larger process that cannot be immediately perceived; the other is usually concrete and immediately perceivable. In your notebook, quickly write down all the analogies that immediately come to mind for the writing process. Then choose several and write out all the points of similarity and difference you can think of between the writing process and the analogy you have selected.

Nan Laurenzio

"Lunchroom Wars" developed from Nan's experiences as a teacher's aide. "Although the actual incident is fictitious, the location of the lunchroom is real and the general characterization of the group is based on children I have known," she says.

"The writing process was interesting in that I clearly saw the comparison from the beginning. My imagination filled in the fictitious details while I placed actual children in the centre of the action. I found myself doing a direct translation in my mind, and somewhere between the thought and the written word I translated children into troops and food into ammunition," Nan explains.

Nan is completing her Bachelor of Arts degree and hopes to pursue a career in teaching.

Lunchroom Wars

I REMEMBER ONE JOB I HAD. My title was Noontime Monitor, but, as I *1*
found out, the responsibilities went well beyond whatever civil implications that rank held. I knew the children I was to monitor, as I had been a teacher's aide in their classroom. They were lovely, eager, fun-loving learners who made the classroom a pleasant experience for me. But my role as noontime monitor was a new venture on foreign turf and I was in for a shock. I was not prepared for the transformation that would take place.

The basement where the lunchroom was located was chilling and gloomy, and descending into the cold, damp depths was like sinking into the trenches in an active battlefield. The cement walls might as well have been the mud embankments of the trenches, and the impermeable cement surroundings resembled the explosive-laden air, everything highly conducive to amplifying even the slightest experimental war cry. This is what happened that day. First one whoop, then an answer, and then the whole room was transformed, as active combat troops began preparing their quarters and collecting their artillery.

I should have been somewhat prepared for what I saw as I entered the *2*
battleground just from the way the sound waves were piercing my eardrums. The normally sweet, soft voices of the children had taken on the tones of reckless rivalry, and screams were pelted out with such force that food and foul language became equally destructive ammunition.

When I peered into the room, tables that at one time had looked fairly domestic, with chairs nicely set around them, had been converted into linoleum blockades, and scattered lunch boxes were the only remains of juvenile civilian life.

3   The blockades were propped so that as many of the troops as possible could crouch in ambush behind the protective barrier. Space was limited in the small room and the opposing cavalry was positioned close enough to the attackers' post that salami, flung at close range, had a superb slapping impact on the target. Ducking just in time, I was witness to the morbid mutilation of a brightly coloured Dole orange bomb as it crashed against the grey barrier and splattered to its soggy death. The hostilities continued and no sooner had a badly bruised banana, oozing from its torn peel, been bombarded in return, than the prized half-full container of Laura Secord's vanilla pudding was hurled back as the final blow. The opponents, temporarily out of ammunition, resorted to war cries that reverberated from the walls, floor, and ceiling and were shot with enough resonance to resemble the Concorde flying low overhead.

4   I was in shock but fortunately my instincts took over and my quiet, calm, tranquil voice was transformed into a captain-in-command howl that I hardly recognized as my own. I was even more surprised to see several sheepish gazes peering out from behind the table tops. I'm not sure if it was the fact that my voice had taken on the fervour of true military control or the fact that both sides seemed to be temporarily out of suitable supplies; either way, the silence that pervaded the room was as annihilating as the havoc that had just ended.

5   If looks could kill, I think I might have won that war. After four curt words from me, the warriors scrambled to reconstruct the room as best their 6-year-old fingers would permit. I retreated into the corridor momentarily to escape the stench of peanut butter and tuna salad, and I could hear an exasperated sigh as one feeble-sounding soldier gasped — probably to himself as much as to any of his cohorts — "I'm friggin' starving." I was never so thankful to hear human expression, such as it was, creeping back into their veteran bodies.

6   Perhaps the environment was mostly to blame for the behaviour I encountered on my first day down in the abyss of the basement-battlefield. But after that day the battle never reached full pitch again. In time those sweet 6-year-olds were to become masters of very refined and subdued activities.

READING

1. Why has this essay been designated an analogy?

2. Is the comparison between a war zone and the lunchroom scene Laurenzio witnessed an appropriate one?

3. This essay is an extended metaphor; once the author likens the lunchroom to a World War I battlefield, she chooses her vocabulary and images accordingly. Choose five typically military words and five images that you particularly like and explain your choices.

4. Does the author effectively sustain the metaphor throughout the essay?

5. Do all paragraphs revolve around war images? If not, which ones do not? What purposes do they serve in the essay?

6. What do you think her "four curt words" in paragraph six were?

7. To which of your five senses does the essay appeal? Give one or two examples of each.

FROM READING TO WRITING

1. Write an essay employing an extended metaphor to describe a common, everyday experience, such as travelling by public transit, registering for classes, walking the dog, or visiting the dentist.

2. Write an essay in which you describe a scene or an incident that impressed you greatly. Try to use vocabulary and images that appeal to the reader's senses of smell, sight, taste, touch, and hearing.

Clint Saulteaux

Clint, of the Nakota/Dakota Nations, was born on Carry-The-Kettle Indian Reserve in southern Saskatchewan and lives in Regina, where he attends the Saskatchewan Indian Federated College. He is enrolled in the Indian Communication Arts program. Clint says that his writing developed as he discovered more about himself. He believes "that all individuals on this planet have a gift of individuality, something to offer someone and everyone else."

Parallel Plains

1   THE BUFFALO ONCE ROAMED the plains of North America. They were a powerful nation, numbering in the tens of millions. They were free to explore the land and to travel great distances. Their diet, which consisted mostly of fresh water and the tall prairie grass, seemed to be supplied by the earth generously. The constant travelling and galloping gave each creature great physical strength. Their only enemy were the human beings, but each encounter was merely another challenge of survival in the larger scheme of things. Each confrontation usually meant a relatively small number of members lost, so a buffalo could usually expect to be reunited with most of his family and his herd. The buffalo, once a proud and mighty nation, lived freely within their environment.

2   Then almost overnight, great changes started occurring. Encounters with the human beings started happening more frequently and with more devastating consequences. These human beings were different from the ones before: they had superior weapons, and they attacked relentlessly, throwing the fear of extermination into the buffalo. There was increasingly less territory to roam. The water was becoming polluted, and the grass was disappearing. Many buffalo remains were left to rot on the earth, causing strange diseases. For the first time, the buffalo experienced the fear of extinction, and it quickly became a predominant fear.

3   Nowadays, the only buffalo remaining are those that live in reserves. They no longer possess the awesome strength they once had because they are now domesticated, like the cows. As a result, they are contracting diseases such as tuberculosis. They no longer experience the fear of being

exterminated by acts of violence; however, their fear of human beings is still prevalent. It is a suppressed, undefined fear.

Many aboriginal people once roamed the plains of North America. 4 They were powerful nations, numbering in the tens of thousands. They were free to explore the land and to become familiar and knowledgeable about how it functioned. As a result, they understood their environment, the ecology, the food chains, and they adapted their lifestyles to maintaining this environment. Their diet consisted mainly of the buffalo, but the buffalo also provided them with shelter, weapons, medicine, clothing, and utensils. So for practical reasons they killed only the number of buffalo that they could use and they left the rest. Their only enemies were other tribes, who may have needed more territory to meet the needs of an increasing number of people within that tribe. However, the wars with other tribes were just another challenge in the daily struggles of living off the land. Many warriors proudly accepted these challenges, knowing they were doing it for the people, and knowing they would be reunited with the people regardless of the outcome.

Then, almost overnight, great changes started occurring. Encounters 5 with the enemies started happening more frequently and with more devastating results. However, the enemy was a different colour of people, and their reasons for warfare were difficult to understand. They were greater in number and they had more powerful weapons, throwing fear of extermination into the Natives. Wave after wave of these new people continued arriving and they demanded more and more land. Soon there was increasingly less territory to live on. The water was becoming polluted, and the grass was disappearing. Diseases started wiping out whole families and villages. For the first time, the aboriginal people started experiencing the fear of genocide, and it became a predominant fear.

Like the buffalo, the Native people were placed on reserves. For 6 many years the reserves broke the spirit of Indians. Diseases such as alcoholism and tuberculosis started occurring rampantly. The Natives were powerless over their predicament and experienced suppression and confusion. Ironically, the reserves may have become the best thing to have happened to Natives. Recently, ceremonies have been revived at an exciting rate. These ceremonies have been functioning without much outside interference due to the isolation of the reserves. The people are getting stronger because of the unity and solidarity due to the isolation of the reserves. Coincidentally, many Native ranchers are looking at the feasibility of raising buffalo herds. Buffalo meat is currently entering the market, and because it is lower in fat and cholesterol and higher in protein, the health-conscious public is eager to try it. As a result both nations, the Natives and the buffalo, will be able to thrive to some degree.

READING

1. What is the significance of the description of the buffalo as a nation in the first paragraph?
2. What was the original state of this nation?
3. Why do you think Saulteaux does not identify the human beings of the second paragraph?
4. In the fourth paragraph, the author describes the original state of the aboriginal nations. How is the first paragraph related to the fourth?
5. How is the second paragraph related to the fifth? How do the last sentences demonstrate this relation?
6. What are the grounds for the analogy between the buffalo and the aboriginal nations?
7. How does the situation described in the final paragraph repeat and transform the situation of the third?
8. How would you define the tone of the essay? Is it effective?

FROM READING TO WRITING

1. An analogy may be used to make concrete something that is abstract or to illustrate the interconnections between two things. Write an essay using an analogy to define a group, community, or nation to which you belong. Begin by writing down all the possible analogies you can create. Then eliminate the possibilities until you discover the most effective one, the analogy with the richest grounds for comparison. Write an essay developing this analogy.

CAUSE AND EFFECT

AUSE AND EFFECT, or causal analysis, is a rhetorical pattern that answers the question *Why*. Most cause and effect essays fall into one of two categories: those that explain causes and those that explain effects or consequences. Occasionally, a writer will choose to explore both causes and effects in one essay, but since this approach entails a complex organization, student essays that focus on one or the other are usually more successful.

A good causal analysis involves a careful examination of complex relationships. You must avoid simplistic reasoning in your attempt to unravel underlying causes. In his essay "Fall from University Grace," Marty J. Chan identifies both the obvious cause of his failure (his neglect of his studies) and the deeper causes (his lack of a career goal, his premature independence, and his immaturity).

In your search for causes or effects, be careful to avoid confusing your reader with too many details. You should make sure that your topic is narrow enough to develop your points adequately within the scope of your essay. Make sure you deal with the most important causes or consequences. If you were writing an essay on the effects of smoking, for example, devoting as much space to yellow fingers and smoky clothes as to lung cancer and emphysema would considerably lessen the impact of your thesis.

In assigning causes to effects, you must strive to be honest, objective, and, above all, rational. Make sure that the causal relationship you have identified is not explained by mere coincidence. One often hears people arguing that an event must have been caused by something that preceded it. ("She went on a roller coaster. That must be why she miscarried.") An absurd example shows the falseness of this reasoning. If John ate a peach half an hour before being hit by a car, does that mean that the peach caused the accident? Be careful about drawing general conclusions from specific instances. Even if you can prove that chewing gum gives you stomachaches, it does not follow that chewing gum is a cause of stomachaches in the general population.

The assertion that all male managers are sexist on the grounds that a female colleague was fired by her male manager exhibits both faulty logic and insufficient evidence. The woman may have been fired for reasons other than her sex; even if that particular manager is sexist, that in itself is no reason to believe that other male managers are.

Make sure your arguments are supported by compelling evidence. If you draw on statistics, make sure they come from a reliable source and that you are using them in context. If you cite a study, make sure it was properly done and that the conclusions drawn follow from the data. Remember that often two studies will result in conflicting evidence.

Cause and effect essays are usually expository or persuasive, although occasionally they make use of personal experience. In its expository form, the cause and effect essay concentrates on an objective statement of causal relationships. In contrast, the persuasive cause and effect essay attempts to convince the reader of the writer's point of view or to provoke the reader to action. Establishing a causal relationship often leads naturally to an argument for action: because draining wetlands disrupts the water table and the wildlife of a region, wetlands should be protected from development; because learning CPR can allow laypeople to save lives, everyone should take a CPR course.

Wayne Atkinson

Wayne is a first-year mature student at Cariboo College. After working as a baker for thirteen years, he returned to school to complete his high-school certificate, but, encouraged by his success, he has decided to continue his education. He is an avid golfer and likens the game to the writing process: "In spite of the frustrations, playing a good round of golf can be very satisfying, and similarly, writing a good paper can be extremely satisfying." While writing this essay, he says, he was "forced to sort out my feelings toward life and ... my priorities." The writing process was, for Wayne, "very therapeutic."

Death: A Warning for the Living

I HAVE, because of the recent and early death of a friend's mother, been 1 dwelling on the whole concept of death, trying to put it into proper perspective. I have tried to find something positive out of something so emotionally devastating. Admittedly, to those currently in despair, and struggling to cope with their grief, the concept that anything positive could come from their recent loss must be incomprehensible. Nevertheless, my experience, both personal and observed, is that death, be it the first taste for youth, the premature demise of the terminally ill, or the first warning for the elderly, is often the catalyst that awakes the living from their apathy.

As a youth I was, like many of my contemporaries, apathetic toward 2 life, and took my time for granted. I had few, if any, thoughts of my own mortality. For almost 30 years, I often took foolish, life-threatening chances, and often justified not doing things by saying I would do them some other day: I had lots of time. During that period, death was something that happened to other people. That was soon to change, however, for death affects all of us eventually. For me, the deaths, in quick succession, of two of my childhood friends changed my philosophy on life forever: I was no longer immortal; I could no longer afford to take senseless chances; I could no longer afford the wasteful habit of procrastination. Death had closed the door on my youthful innocence forever; death forced me to take life seriously, to make the most of life and, at least, try to live out the dreams I had.

3   The plight of the terminally ill, though tragic, can, in specific cases such as AIDS, cause positive changes in the victims. Although it may be difficult to imagine anything positive about having this disease, AIDS can, and does, have a positive effect on some victims' attitudes toward life. Because the disease is often diagnosed years before it is fatal, AIDS gives the victims time to re-evaluate their lives. A recent TV documentary focussed on an inner-city youth who acquired the virus from intravenous drug abuse, and although a tragedy by his own admission, AIDS was the best thing that has happened to him. After many years of self-centredness, self-destructiveness, and self-pity, he was transformed by the stark reality of his impending demise. As a result, he learned to give instead of to take, to be positive instead of negative. He became determined, for the remainder of his healthy years, to live life in a constructive manner.

4   For many elderly people, the thoughts of death are often cause for apathy and depression. They are often despondent through lack of focus during the idle years of retirement, and sometimes only a brush with death can snap them out of their listlessness. A good example is a neighbour of mine who, after suffering a series of heart attacks and subsequent by-pass operation, had a remarkable change in his outlook. One of his greatest passions in life was, and is, the care of his backyard garden, and it was there, during a recent conversation with him, I noticed the change in his attitude. He seemed to be fixated on the mysteries of life and on the life force of the whole yard, which in the early spring was becoming so evident. He spoke in awe of the sprouting vegetables, the flowering fruit trees, and of the budding ornamental flowers. But, above all, the discovery of a grub on one of his trees convinced me his attitude had changed, for upon discovery of the grub, he commented on the complexity of life in the grub, and then let it continue on its way. Before the heart attacks, he likely would have crushed the grub the moment he saw it. No longer did he believe himself to be the omnipotent master of his garden, but more an equal partner in a complex environment. His close brush with death seemed to free him from his narrow vision that was full of self-pity and apathy. This new-found clarity seemed to give him contentment.

5   Life is cyclical by nature, and death is a natural part of it, but we often push the thought of our death to the back of our conscious mind. Nevertheless, the sands of time flow continuously for all of us, and if anything positive can be said of death, it is that death often serves as a warning bell that awakes the survivors from apathy and pushes them into taking their first steps toward fulfilling their dreams, desires, and aspirations, while they still have time.

READING

1. Sentences should flow logically and naturally from one to the next. How do the four sentences of the first paragraph demonstrate the process of cause and effect?

2. Consult the section on the thesis statement in "The Writing Process." Which sentence functions as Atkinson's thesis statement? Does this sentence fulfil all the requirements of the successful thesis statement?

3. The form or structure of an essay, paragraph, or sentence should demonstrate the content. How does the construction of the sixth sentence of the second paragraph (beginning "For me, the deaths ...") demonstrate the sequence of cause and effect?

4. What are the parallels between the second and the third examples in paragraphs three and four? Compare and contrast the last four sentences (beginning "Before the heart attacks ...") especially.

5. Why do you think the author presents these three examples in this order?

6. How does the last paragraph connect with and complete the first paragraph?

7. What tone does the author strike in this essay? How is it appropriate to his topic?

FROM READING TO WRITING

1. The great events of birth and death naturally have a great effect on people's lives. Think of smaller events, serious or comic, that also cause people to re-evaluate their lives. Choose one of these and discover as many examples as you can. Then select two or three appropriate examples and write an essay outlining the process of cause and effect.

2. Think of other cause and effect relationships — physical, political, economic, etc. Isolate a particular effect that you wish to discuss — the symptoms of stress, the decline in public trust of governments, the growth of third world debt, etc. List as many possible causes as you can. Then try to discover the most plausible cause, and write an essay demonstrating the relation of cause and effect.

Marty J. Chan

"Discipline is the key to writing," observes Marty. "I found that forcing myself to sit and write, rather than waiting for inspiration, allowed me to write with more precision. The key is to read and rewrite your work over and over until you are sure it says what you mean."

Marty also finds that "writing about simple experiences is the most effective way of writing well." Marty has written numerous murder mystery scripts and short stories. He hopes to work as a free-lance writer, director, and actor.

Fall from University Grace

1   JUST AS ADAM WAS CAST OUT OF EDEN, I was kicked out of university; but while his transgression was eating the fruit from the tree of knowledge, my sin was ignoring the tree. After my dismal performance in my first year of university, I contemplated the reasons for my failure. Now, I understand the two factors that contributed to my downfall: the lack of a career goal and premature independence.

2   Without a career goal, I lacked direction and motivation. About halfway through my final year of high school, I was hounded by my parents to enrol in university, but until that time I had not given any thought to what career I wanted to pursue. Two of my friends were already in the engineering program at university, so, to silence my parents' nagging, I told them that I wanted to be an engineer. In retrospect, I realize that this was a big mistake. Though I got high marks in math, physics, and chemistry — core courses of the engineering program — I was bored with them, and my dislike of the sciences became apparent in the first four months of university. I failed all science courses.

3   Had I been more motivated, I might have passed those courses, but I just wasn't ready for university; in fact, I wasn't ready for any career. I assumed that the amount of studying I did in high school — an hour per day — would be sufficient to attain respectable marks in university. I was wrong. After the first two weeks, I realized I had to study more, but I couldn't confine myself to a desk for longer than an hour. Because I could not see myself as an engineer, I could not motivate myself to study harder; then I began looking for excuses to avoid studying.

Before study sessions, I often wandered around the library for half an 4
hour, looking for just the right carrel in which to study. When I finally
found my niche, I left my backpack, unopened, on the chair and I went to
the arcade in a nearby mall. My excuse for doing this was that I needed
inspiration to study dull formulas; I believed playing *Space Invaders* would
help. It didn't. Two hours later, I returned to the carrel, took my backpack, left the library, and went home.

Even when I was reading my textbooks, I wasn't studying. Daydreams 5
of sleeping on a patch of cool grass on a breezy summer day intruded upon
my concentration, chasing away calculus and physics theories. By the
time the daydreams ended, I had forgotten most of what I had studied in
the previous hour. As the midterm week drew closer, the daydreams grew
longer while the study sessions grew shorter. Studying was avoidable as
long as daydreaming was possible. I escaped often and as a result I failed
my math, chemistry, and physics exams.

Why didn't I transfer to another program? Why didn't I just drop out? 6
First, my parents had paid for my tuition and I feared they would pull out
their financial support and leave me destitute. Second, my aspirations
were still cloudy, so if I transferred out of the engineering faculty I would
still lack direction. Without a definite goal, afraid of disappointing my
strict parents, I remained in the program until Christmas, hopeful that my
marks would improve as well as my disposition toward engineering.

However, passing grades eluded me, as did maturity. Coming from a 7
small town and being unaccustomed to the fast-paced routine of campus
life, I inhabited the residence hall, believing that it would shelter me from
competitive courses and merciless engineering professors. After the first
month of adjustment, I learned that the place offered the niceties of home
without the watchful eye of parents. Also, I found other students who felt
just as unhappy as I did, and we complained for hours in the local pub
about the emotional wounds university professors inflicted on below-
average students.

Snow fell in mid-December — final exam time — but I didn't notice 8
either event, because I had become a creature of the night, preying on full
beer mugs in smoke-filled bars. A week later, snow covered every building
on campus, which promised a white Christmas for everyone but me: my
exams had been returned and the test scores were so low that if I added all
four marks together, they amounted to one grade of any average student. I
didn't care; neither did my friends, who received similar marks. We
bragged of our freedom from our parents, not realizing that their influence
was more beneficial than the influence we had on each other.

When my friends and I were not in the bar, we were playing cards in 9
somebody's room or inviting ourselves to private parties held by other students in the residence hall. It never failed that, at least twice a night,

someone would knock on my door in an attempt to lure me into a card game or to cajole me into accompanying him to the bar. Every Thursday, a game of hockey took place in my hallway and, feeling obligated, I left my studies and played in goal. On weekends, we became warriors determined to prove our stamina by consuming dozens of bottles of beer — I had lost every battle — followed by marathon vomiting contests, of which I had won many.

10   At the time, my independence was exhilarating; freedom, denied me for eighteen years, was mine to experience and abuse. I got drunk with impunity. No angry mother awaited my return home at five in the morning. No enraged father tongue lashed me for lousy grades. I was self-reliant. But freedom had its price: nobody told me to study harder; no one said that if I didn't get an 80 on my next three exams, I would fail; no one told me to take responsibility for my actions. I answered to no one but myself. I was self-reliant; I was an ass.

11   When Christmas day arrived, I found a "withdraw from university" notice in my stocking. My refusal to claim responsibility for my actions and my abuse of newly gained independence and freedom from parental rule had combined to ensure my marks were below the passing grade and to make my Christmas black.

12   Unearned independence was the fruit from the tree of knowledge that tempted me and caused my downfall. Because I was not mature enough to accept the responsibility for my own future and because I abused my privileges of independence, I failed my first year of university. The causes of my downfall have taught me maturity and responsibility, and in the future, I will not ignore the tree of knowledge again. Falling from Eden was enough to teach Adam; the same is true for me.

READING

1. What is Chan's thesis? Is it explicit or implied? Does the organization of the essay reflect his thesis statement?

2. Do you think that the metaphor of Adam's fall from grace is an apt one to describe the author's experience? Why or why not?

3. Does the author sustain the biblical metaphor throughout the essay?

4. Does his procrastination strike any familiar chords in you? If so, in what ways?

5. What influence did Chan's friends have on him? Why do you think he chose to fraternize with them?

6. Who is the intended audience?

7. Remember that different essay types are not completely exclusive categories. For example, descriptive elements may appear in any other kind of essay. What other rhetorical elements do you find in this essay?

8. Punctuation marks are used for different purposes, among them emphasis, direction, and clarity. Chan employs a variety of punctuation marks in paragraph eight. Which ones does he choose? Does he use them correctly?

9. The author concludes that, like Adam, he learned his lesson. Do you believe him? Why or why not?

FROM READING TO WRITING

1. Keep a record of one week's study sessions. How many hours do you really study? How often does your mind wander? How often do you take a trip to the refrigerator? What do you do when you get tired of studying? Write an essay giving examples of your personal patterns of study avoidance.

2. Interview a student whom you consider successful. Choose someone who not only maintains an acceptable grade-point average but also has accomplishments in some other field, whether it be varsity athletics, student government, the arts, or community service. Find out how this student manages his or her time, sets priorities, and establishes short-term and long-term goals. Write an essay reflecting the answers to your interview questions.

Michele Landsberg

Michele Landsberg is a Canadian author and columnist with a special concern for family and women's issues. Her columns have appeared in The Globe and Mail *and* The Toronto Star. *This essay appears in her volume* Women and Children First *(1982).*

Ceremonies

1   CEREMONIES — weddings, christenings, bar mitzvahs, graduations, and even, heaven help me, birthdays and parades — always make me cry.

2   "Now snap out of this sentimental idiocy." I told myself, in what I imagined to be my best Bella Abzug growl, as I sat at the McMaster University convocation last Friday. No use, I felt the old familiar sting under the eyelids as the fanfare rang out, the academics solemnly paraded in their multicoloured gowns, the beaming parents sat tier on tier in the bleachers of what is normally a gym, and the "graduands" began to file endlessly past the chancellor to receive their degrees.

3   Now, in serene ceremony, three or four undignified years (heady new freedom, intellectual passion, beery hangovers, stomach-churning exams) were signed and sealed in dignity. In their hundreds, the young graduands (so much shining hair, so many scrubbed faces) came in an unwinding ribbon of black gowns to kneel before Chancellor Allan Leal. "I admit you Bachelor of Arts," he said to each one, and not even after the 200th did his voice lose its cheery boom of congratulation. Then the academic hood (like a long loop of silk-scarf) was slipped over his or her shoulders, and the young graduate turned to march down from the podium and into the world.

4   In the moment of turning, student after student beamed at us a tremendous, exultant, partly embarrassed smile, lips closed so that they wouldn't burst into an involuntary laugh of delight. And each one, striding down the aisle, sought out his or her family in the crowd to exchange a glance of triumph.

5   Why do moments like that make people cry? The parents of the graduates, of course, have the excitement of pride to justify their moist eyes. But even for bystanders like me, there's an irresistible poignancy about ceremonies. I first started to feel that way in my teens, when it dawned on

Example   155

me that summer did not last forever, and that next year was always turning into this year, and then fading into last year with startling speed.

I began to hoard life the way other people hoard elastic bands or vintage 6 wines, latching onto anything which slowed down the quicksilver passage of time. In my mental bank account, I have a peculiar half-conscious ledger system for keeping track of time won and lost. I hate to sleep in, because that steals away part of the day, and I hate to go to sleep at night. I love summer because the days are long and crammed with the sensual treasures which I stockpile in memory against the turn of the year. A day spent picking raspberries in the hot sun is a day wrestled away from the black hole of eternity. But an afternoon spent in a movie is an afternoon lost forever, an afternoon which trickled away while I wasn't there.

I gloat over anything ancient — words, or Roman coins, or human 7 rituals — because they have been scooped up and saved from the obliterating flood of time. I once seized on and saved a tattered, yellowing handwritten title deed to a Muskoka log cabin whose ruins I was exploring. And I memorized the flowers still growing in the dooryard; someone had planted them, once. In France, I spent some happy hours exulting over the name of a river, a name which, according to the books, had come down from pre-history. Imagine: a one-syllable word had survived since before recorded time.

Ceremonies conquer time, too, and I suppose that's why I love them. 8 Participants in ceremony seem to me to step out of time for the moment. Caveboys and cavegirls must have smiled just this way (new dignity struggling with exuberance) when they passed their test of adulthood and went forth from the parental cave.

Weddings, funerals, harvest festivals, and religious rites which have 9 come unchanged through the centuries, all snatch us up from the rush of time and hold us still, linked to those who have felt these feelings before and those who will feel them after we have died.

So I forgave myself for my "sentimental idiocy" at the McMaster con- 10 vocation. And I only smiled tolerantly when I saw my children rolling their eyes at each other in mock exasperation to tease me for my weakness. Just the way, come to think of it, I used to tease my own mother ... while wondering a little uneasily what it was that adults knew, what it was that made them blink away tears at ceremonial moments sad and gay.

READING

1. What do the ceremonies in the list in Landsberg's first sentence all have in common?

2. How do the first two sentences of the third paragraph express the difference between daily student life and the solemn pageantry of the graduation? How are the sentences similar and different?

3. How does the author make the transition from the focus on the graduation in the first five paragraphs to the discussion of ceremonies in general in the last five?

4. What figurative language does she use in the sixth paragraph to account for her response to her realization in the fifth paragraph?

5. Do the two examples of paragraph seven belong together? How are they similar and different?

6. In this essay, Landsberg is discovering and expressing emotional cause and effect or affect, as it is properly called. Why do ceremonies make people cry?

7. What does she mean when she writes that "participants in ceremony seem to me to step out of time for the moment"?

8. How does the conclusion of the essay connect with the introduction? What does this connection express about ceremonies?

FROM READING TO WRITING

1. We have all taken part in ceremonies, both as participants and as observers. Recall a ceremony that you participated in or observed, and write a short essay describing the affect it had on you and others.

2. New forms of technology usually have a great effect on our lives. Choose a particular technological innovation that has appeared in your lifetime or that particularly interests you and write a short essay discussing its effects on you and others.

4

Persuasive Writing

What I like in a good writer
is not what he says, but
what he whispers.

– Logan Pearsall Smith

Every detail should be important:
a single blade of grass
should be as clear to your
reader as a main character.

– Robert L. Newman
(student essayist)

INTRODUCTION

P ERSUASIVE WRITING goes one step further than expository writing. In a persuasive essay, you strive not only to explain your thesis clearly to your reader but also to convince your reader to agree with your point of view. Often, persuasive essays attempt to convince the reader to take some course of action.

Thus, everything we said in Part 3 about the importance of structure, logic, and discipline in the expository essay applies doubly to the persuasive essay. Where a descriptive piece can be free flowing, concentrating more on mood than on the exact information conveyed, an expository essay must be organized logically to allow the reader to follow the author's reasoning. In a persuasive essay, you need to lay out your ideas and the evidence that supports them so clearly that the reader not only follows your reasoning but is carried along inexorably from point to point and comes to the same conclusion that you do. Each plank of your argument must be laid carefully on the last, building a strong edifice that can stand up to examination and counter-argument.

ARGUMENT

A N ARGUMENT IS A REASON or line of reasoning put forth to convince someone of the correctness of your opinion. As part of this effort, you have to confront and refute opposing opinions. Your tools are logical thought and the clear presentation of firm evidence. Trying to arouse the audience's emotions through loaded words or reference to irrelevant but emotionally charged situations is not argument but just cheap manipulation. This is not to say it will never work: many people have won personal arguments and many politicians have swayed crowds by such tactics. However, appealing to the emotions will backfire with an intelligent audience that can see through it. Moreover, this approach is never justified: if your opinion is correct, it can be supported by reason.

Examples of argument are all around us in our daily lives; but much of the argument we hear is flawed, lacking in organization, poorly structured, and more emotional than reasoned.

Example: How Not to Argue

As a simple example, let us imagine you are tired of living at home and would like to share an apartment with a friend. However, you would like your parents' permission and need their financial support. How do you go about convincing them that you are worthy of the opportunity?

Knowing your parents as well as you do, do you think any of the following arguments will work?

1. All my friends have their own apartments.

2. If you say No, you don't love me.

3. If you don't give permission, I'll stop eating.

4. It'll be much cheaper if I move out.

5. Albert Einstein had his own apartment and he got good grades.

6. I'll take another part-time job to help pay the rent.

The answer to the previous question is probably a resounding No. Statement number one is unlikely to be true; it is, rather, a sloppy generalization. Number two is a ridiculous attempt to play on your parents' emotions (though, if you repeat it often enough and if they are emotionally vulnerable, they may believe it). Number three is an improbable threat. Number four is implausible: although expenses in your parents' home may indeed decrease, the additional expenses of rent, utilities, and food at your apartment will undoubtedly outweigh any savings. Number five so obviously proves nothing (even if it is true) that it will just send your parents' gaze skyward. Number six may inadvertently give your parents another reason to refuse your request.

A More Reasoned Argument

If you are convinced of your desire and ability to share an apartment, you will have to give more thought to the process of gaining your parents' consent. In the first place, you will avoid any statements that will indicate to your parents that you are immature (numbers two and three), exaggerating (number one), illogical (numbers four and five), or unrealistic (number six). In addition, you will first anticipate their views, formulate their counter-arguments, and develop logical replies (refutations) before voicing your own.

Your parents may bring up the following points:

1. Your best friend Dana failed two courses after moving out of the parental home.

2. You are too young to live so independently.

3. We'll miss you terribly.

4. The additional cost is prohibitive.

You might refute point number one by reminding them that your grades have always been higher than Dana's, and you have never yet been in danger of failing a course. To refute number two, you can list your responsible behaviour to date in all aspects of your school and home life. You may have to promise to phone or visit at least once a week to put concern number three to rest. Point number four requires the most thoughtful response. You may have to repeat your impeccable record of responsible behaviour as in refutation number two and call on their trust in you to repay them from your earnings from the two jobs you intend to take in the summer. If you address your parents' concerns logically and unemotionally, you will stand a much better chance of convincing them to agree to your proposal.

An argument essay is, of course, a more formal expression of your point of view. As such, it must follow stricter rules to be effective.

What Makes an Argument Essay Effective?

To be effective, an argument essay must have a clearly stated thesis. You cannot afford to divide your focus. For example, "The women's movement in Canada has improved the status of the average woman in some ways, while in others it has actually damaged the pre-existing status." You will not find many readers willing to follow the winding path of any essay that could possibly result from such a weak thesis.

What do you do if this is what you actually believe? The easiest solution is to choose one side or the other: argue that the women's movement has benefited women or that it has harmed them. Another possibility is to abandon the topic altogether and write about something on which your beliefs are more black and white. However, there is a way to be honest to your ambivalent feelings and still write a convincing essay. Give some hard thought to your reasons for writing the essay and narrow your focus. For example, suppose you believe that the women's movement has benefited women in the workplace but has damaged the status of women who choose to stay home with their children. You might decide to write a piece aimed at a feminist audience. Your new thesis could be "The women's movement has isolated and stigmatized the stay-at-home mother; feminists should reach out to these women and support them in their chosen lifestyle." You could have one paragraph, subordinated to the overall argument, in which you state your general support for the women's movement and its achievements.

Once you have arrived at a thesis statement worthy of your essay, you must decide the order in which you will present your refutations and arguments. This order may vary, depending on the subject of your essay. In most cases, however, your refutation of anticipated counter-arguments will come first. Then you will state your arguments from weakest to strongest; or perhaps you will begin with your second strongest argument, state the others in descending order of strength, and end with your strongest argument. All your arguments must be sound and convincing; "weak" does not mean irrelevant or invalid.

As in all formal writing, a strong introduction, conclusion, and state-ment of background (if necessary) are essential. In addition to these elements, an essay of argument/persuasion will often require outside evidence as support. Be prepared to research your topic thoroughly and to use appropriate facts, statistics, or examples to back up your thesis. (Of course, you will document your sources.)

Finally, as we mentioned earlier, you must argue your points logically and fairly, not by appealing to emotion. This obligation does not mean that your essay must be completely unfeeling. The legitimate route to your readers' emotions is through making them aware of information that is in itself moving. For example, if you quoted factual descriptions from case studies of children suffering from a debilitating disease and then gave sound medical evidence that a certain technique would prevent it, you wouldn't need to use inflammatory language to arouse your readers' com-passion for the children or anger against anything that blocked use of the technique.

In addition, of course, never tamper with facts. You may get away with it in the short run, if you are lucky, but in the long run you will be found out and will lose all credibility.

Any good handbook of English contains examples of faulty logic and irresponsible argument. Consult one for a more detailed explanation. As a matter of course, though, argue your point of view the way you would want to have an opposing position presented to you. Use fairness and reliable support to argue for your thesis.

Dina Amicone

Dina is interested in history, sociology, the history and identity of Canada's ethnic communities, and the concept of multiculturalism. She likes to read historical novels, humour and satire, biographies, and contemporary novels. As a recent graduate with a Bachelor of Arts degree, she is looking forward to a career in French–English translation.

Dina believes that good writing is like an interesting conversation: it must express ideas in a clear and simple way. "Just as the tone of voice and emphasis on certain words add life to conversation, so, too, the structure, tone, mood, and organization of ideas into a logical progression make for enjoyable reading," she observes.

In Defence of the Secretary

1   NO JOB HAS BEEN subjected to as much ridicule as that of the secretary. The media stereotype secretaries as big busted, scatter-brained young women sitting around the office filing their nails, or rude, uppity spinsters well past their prime.

2   The women's movement has helped to change attitudes and improve conditions, but not the secretary's. She has become an embarrassment to many liberationists who view the role as the last bastion of male domination. As a result, secretaries are often unwilling to admit to being "just a secretary," and many are now changing their titles to "administrative assistant" or "administrative agent."

3   Recently, however, with the advent of computer technology, some people have begun to argue that we secretaries are at a crossroads. Many believe that the new technology will give us power over our bosses and help correct problems such as lack of appreciation, too much pressure, and low pay. The computer is a marvellous piece of working equipment, but it is foolish to believe it will give us the recognition we deserve.

4   Those who argue that the computer will help our condition feel that secretaries, with their new-found computer skills, could now control a firm's information. This control is supposedly an ace in our deck, which we can use to gain recognition and revise our job descriptions in order to become technicians and administrators.

5   In most offices, however, the acquisition of a computer has not brought about a change in the secretary's job description, except that now

she sits in front of a screen all day, instead of a typewriter, and is expected to turn out more work.

Some have also put forth the idea that bosses are now dependent on 6 their subordinates and feel threatened because they are ignorant of this new technology. This implies that we should somehow take advantage of their ignorance.

Many bosses do not know the first thing about word processing, but a 7 secretary can by no means use this as ammunition. Bosses have never known how to type or use telex machines, yet they have always had the upper hand. How could a computer make the situation any different? Unfortunately, most bosses, unfamiliar with the workings of a computer, believe that the work will get done instantaneously. A former boss once asked me to change the margins on a financial statement I had on disk. When I did so and the neat rows of figures became disaligned, I and several other secretaries told him the numbers had to be pushed back into place, one by one. Mr. Boss couldn't believe that the software program he'd paid so much for didn't have a "fix margin" button that could correct the problem quickly, especially since he'd invested the extra money for that extensive day-long course he'd had me take!

Computer enthusiasts refer to their technology and our know-how as 8 an adventure in which we secretaries will rise up, diskette in hand, and hold the information we control ransom for better job descriptions. If most secretaries I know tried this tactic, they'd likely find themselves holding their walking papers. Bosses don't want a rebel for a secretary. For many bosses, a secretary must be efficient, co-operative, and, above all, cheerful. They expect her to stay on after five to finish that report, keep smiling while doing so, and not ask for overtime compensation. These efforts on her part are, at times, well rewarded by Mr. Boss: at Christmas, a bottle of perfume; on Valentine's Day, a box of chocolates; not to mention Secretary's Week, when he shows his appreciation with roses and lunch, although a raise would be more in order.

What those who extol the merits of the computer neglect to consider 9 is the bosses. Maybe the computer will take care of them too! Some people are fascinated by computers. It is a great thrill for the writer to punch in an article and watch the revisions on the screen, or for the composer to use a computer to write a fugue, but for the word processing operator, typing report after report, who is expected to meet a daily quota, the novelty of modern technology soon wears off. Even if employers did spend some money on programs to help workers adapt to computers, a person whose eyes are riveted to a screen for seven hours is bound to suffer eyestrain, neck aches, and even depression.

There is no escaping the fact that the role of the secretary is to deal 10 with those things her boss doesn't have time for. There will always be telephones to answer and reports to type. A computer might allow us to do these tasks faster, but why pretend it will revolutionize our jobs?

11   We secretaries shouldn't receive better pay or recognition simply because we can use a computer. This notion is insulting and negates everything else we do. Do architects or accountants make more money because they can now use a computer to help them?

12   No, the computer is just a tool. Secretaries must use language and grammar correctly, take notes, understand the principles of publishing and presentation of documents, manage time, and possess huge amounts of diplomacy and tact. Few people ever stop to think about the know-how involved in producing a neat, concise, and accurate report or letter.

13   Most bosses often hand in a sloppy, mistake riddled, almost illegible handwritten draft and casually mention that you should "feel free" to correct any spelling or grammar mistakes. These are often the same bosses who will reason that their secretaries are overpaid for the "light typing" they do. I wonder what would happen if secretaries began leaving the mistakes in.

14   A friend of mine recently fell upon one boss who understood all too well that secretaries want to be treated as professionals. "We're all equal here," he told her the day she was hired. As a "professional" in a public relations firm, she was expected to work till 2:00 A.M. to finish typing presentations, with no overtime pay, since professionals receive remuneration on an annual basis. The hitch was, however, that she was the only "professional" expected to come in at 9:00 the next morning to man the phones and prepare a continental breakfast for the others who would saunter in at 11:00, bleary-eyed, asking her to "be a doll and fetch a cup of coffee."

15   Secretaries are the unsung heroes because the profession has remained, by and large, a female one, just as nursing and teaching were, before an influx of men brought these professions more respectability and better pay. That the secretarial profession could use both goes without saying.

16   There is no reason an experienced secretary, knowledgeable in computers or not, who works for the City of Montreal, for example, should make four dollars less per hour than a newly hired blue-collar worker. Computers won't change the work camp atmosphere. Calling us administrative assistants won't. Equal pay for work of equal value will.

READING

1. Who is Amicone's intended audience?

2. What is her thesis? Is it explicit or implied? At what point in the essay does it appear?

3. Is the introductory paragraph effective in grabbing the reader's attention? Why or why not?

4. Reread paragraphs four through nine. List the counter-arguments the author considers and refutes before expressing her own opinions.

5. Do you think she refutes the counter-arguments fairly, logically, and effectively? Why or why not?

6. In which paragraph(s) do you think the author presents her most convincing argument(s)? Explain your choice(s).

7. In what ways is a secretary "rewarded" for her word processing skills?

8. Is the concluding paragraph an appropriate and effective one to end this essay? Why or why not?

FROM READING TO WRITING

1. Think of a job that is traditionally done by women. Describe the responsibilities of the job. Why is it one that is considered "women's work"? Formulate a thesis that states the "gender designation" of the job. Write an essay explaining this designation and expressing your reactions to it.

2. Follow the steps listed in the preceding question but choose a job that is traditionally done by men.

Ken Dryden

Ken Dryden, a native of Hamilton, Ontario, was a star goaltender for the Montreal Canadiens for eight seasons. He was selected to the all-star team and won the Vezina Trophy for outstanding goalie five times. He also won the Conn Smythe Trophy as the most valuable player in the playoff in his rookie year. This essay is reprinted from The Game *(1983).*

The Game

1   ONCE I USED TO WAIT IN LINE like everyone else. Then one day a bank teller motioned Me out of the line, and I haven't been back in one since. I feel no small guilt each time; nonetheless I continue to accept such favours. For the tellers and me, it has become normal and routine. They treat me the way they think people like me expect to be treated. And I accept.

2   It is the kind of special treatment professional athletes have grown accustomed to, and enjoy. It began with hockey, with teenage names and faces in local papers, with hockey jackets that only the best players on the best teams wore, with parents who competed not so quietly on the side; and it will end with hockey. In between, the longer and better we play the more all-encompassing the treatment becomes. People give, easily and naturally. And we accept. Slippers, sweaters, plant holders, mitts, baby blankets, baby clothes sent in the mail. Paintings, carvings, etchings, sculptures in clay, metal, papier-mâché. Shirts, slacks, coats, suits, ties, underwear; cars, carpets, sofas, chairs, refrigerators, beds, washers, dryers, stoves, TVs, stereos, at cost or no cost at all. After all, a special person deserves a special price. A hundred letters a week, more than 3,000 a year — "You're the best," all but a few of them say. On the street, in restaurants and theatres, we're pointed at, talked about like the weather. "There he is, the famous hockey player," your own kids announce to their friends. In other homes, your picture is on a boy's bedroom wall. Magazines, newspapers, radio, TV; hockey cards, posters, T-shirts, and curios, anywhere, everywhere, name, face, thousands of times.

3   And we love it. We say we don't, but we do. We hate the nuisance and inconvenience, the bother of untimely, unending autographs, handshakes, and smiles, living out an image of ourselves that isn't quite real,

abused if we fail to, feeling encircled and trapped, never able to get away. But we also feel special — head-turning, chin-dropping, forget-your-name special. What others buy Rolls-Royces and votes and hockey teams for, what others take off their clothes for, what others kill for, we have. All we have to do is play.

If exposure is the vehicle of celebrity, attention is what separates one 4 celebrity from another. Guy Lafleur and Yvon Lambert are both celebrities, yet on the same ice, the same screen, Lafleur is noticed, Lambert is not. Lambert, methodical and unspectacular, has nothing readily distinctive about him. His image is passed over, his name unheard. Lafleur *is* distinctive. The way he skates, the sound of the crowd he carries with him, the goals he scores.

And so, too, others, for other reasons. Mario Tremblay, for his fiery, 5 untamed spirit; Bob Gainey, for his relentless, almost palpable will; Tiger Williams, Eddie Shack, Ron Duguay, each colourful and exciting; and Dave Schultz, once king of the mountain. As sports coverage proliferates beyond games, as it becomes entertainment and moves to prime time, as we look for the story behind the story, off-ice performance becomes important. And so personas are born, and sometimes made, and cameras and microphones are there as it happens. The crazies, the clowns, the "sports intellectuals," the anti-jock rebels (Jim Bouton, Bill "Spaceman" Lee), the playboys (Joe Namath, Derek Sanderson), each a distinctive personality, each a bigger celebrity because of what he does away from the game.

TV has given us a new minimum off-ice standard. The modern player 6 must be articulate (or engagingly inarticulate, especially southern style). It's not enough to score a goal and have it picked apart by the all-seeing eyes of replay cameras. A player must be able to put it in his own eloquent words. How did you do it? How did you feel? Live, on-camera words that cannot be edited for the morning paper.

Celebrity is a full, integrated life, earned on-ice, performed, sustained, 7 strengthened, re-earned off-ice. As Roger Angell once put it, we want our athletes to be "good at life." Role models for children, people we want to believe earned what they have, every bit as good at things off the ice as on. If they're inarticulate, harsh and pejorative, they're suddenly just jocks. Merely lucky, less likable, less good at life, less celebrated; finally, they even seem less good *on* the ice.

At its extreme, the process creates the category of professional celebri- 8 ty, people "famous for being famous," so accomplished at being celebrities that their original source of deity is forgotten. At the least, it encourages all celebrities to learn the *skills* of the public person. How to look good, how to sound modest and intelligent, funny and self-deprecatory, anything you want. It's a celebrity's short-cut to the real thing, but it works.

Walter Cronkite *looks* trustworthy, Ronald Reagan seems like a nice guy, Denis Potvin *sounds* intelligent; or is he only articulate? Good enough at something to be a public person, or simply a good public person? You'll never get close enough long enough to know.

9   All around us are people anxious to help us look better. Not just flacks and PR types but a whole industry of journalists, commentators, biographers, award-givers. Ghost-writers who put well-paid words under our names, then disappear; charity organizers, volunteers who give time and effort so that "honorary presidents" and "honorary directors" may look even better. Children in hospitals, old folks in old folks' homes — we autograph their casts, shake their hands, make them props to our generosity and compassion. And never far away, photographers and cameramen record the event. It is the bandwagon momentum of celebrityhood.

10   In the end, for us, is an image. After thousands of confused messages, we cut through what is complex and render it simple. One image, concrete and disembodied. What agents call "Ken Dryden."

11   Recently, I asked an executive at an advertising agency to pretend he was trying to persuade a client to use me as a commercial spokesman for his company. We'd met two or three times, several years before, so he knew me mostly as others do. He wrote the following memo to his client: "Historically I know you have some concerns about using an athlete ... either because of potential problems developing out of their careers and public life, or due to simply their lack of availability. I think Ken is quite different from the rest. He is known as a thoughtful, articulate and concerned individual. I think it would go without saying he would not participate in any endorsation unless he was fully committed to and satisfied with the product. (His Ralph Nader exposures would assure that.) He is serious, respected and appears to be very much his own man. I don't think we could ever consider using him in humorous or light approaches (like Eddie Shack) unless it would be by juxtaposition with another ... actor or player. He has good media presence. ... His physical presence is also commanding. He is quite tall and impressive. ... Other encouraging things would be his intelligence and educational background. He would be more in tune with our target audience with his credentials as a college graduate (Cornell) and a fledgling professional person (law). Also, during production, I think this intelligence and coolness would help in case of commercial production as well as helping to keep costs under control due to mental errors. ..."

12   So that's my image. Is it accurate? It doesn't matter. It's what people think, it presupposes how they'll react to me. And for the ad man and his client, how people will react is what matters.

13   If I don't like my image, I can do something about it. I can do things that are "good for my image." I can stop doing things that are "bad for my

image." As actors remind us casually and often, I can do things to change my image. Is it too serious? If I run around the dressing room throwing water at the right moment, someone is bound to notice. A journalist with a dead-line to meet and space to fill, a new angle, news — "Dryden misunderstood."

Want to be known as an antique collector? Collect an antique. A the- 14 atre-goer? Go. Once is enough. Tell a journalist, sound enthusiastic, and, above all, play well. Then stand back and watch what happens. Clipped and filed, the news spreads like a chain letter, to other journalists who don't have time to check it out. Presto, it's part of your standard bio. And your image.

If you substitute the work "reputation" for "image," as you might have 15 done a few years ago, you'd have something quite different. A reputation is nothing so trifling or cynical. Like an old barge, it takes time to get going. It's slow and relentless, difficult to manoeuvre, even harder to stop. An image is nothing so solemn. It is merely a commercial asset, a package of all the rights and good-will associated with "Ken Dryden" — some-thing I can sell to whomever I want.

But it's a sticky matter. For the image I'm selling is *your* image of me. 16 The good-will, though it relates to me, is your good-will. Whatever com-mercial value there is in my name, my image, it's you who puts it there. You like me or trust me, and any prospective buyer of my image, anxious to put my name alongside his product, knows that and counts on it to make you buy his product. And you might, even though it may not be in your best interest. So by selling my name, I have perhaps taken your trust and turned it against you.

I did a commercial once, six years ago. I'd decided I never would, but 17 this one was different enough to start a web of rationalizations until I for-got the point and accepted. A fast-food chain was looking for a winter promotion; Hockey Canada, the advisory and promotional body, wanted a fundraiser and a way to deliver the message to kids and their parents that minor hockey can be approached and played differently. The idea was a mini-book done by Hockey Canada, then sold through the restaurant chain. I was to be a collaborator on the book, and its public spokesman. But after doing the TV and radio ads (for the book, but with a corporate jingle at the end), and seeing the point-of-purchase cardboard likenesses of me in the restaurant, I realized my mistake.

Since then, I have turned down endorsements for, among other 18 things, a candy bar ("The way I see it, a full body shot of you in the net, mask up, talking, then we draw in tight on your catching glove, you open it, the bar's inside ..."), a credit card company ("You may not know me without my mask, but ..."), and a roll-on deodorant that would also be promoted by several other people whose names begin with the sound "dry."

19   It's a game — an ad game, an image game, a celebrity game — that no one really loses. Everyone needs someone to talk about — why not about us? Everyone needs heroes and villains. We earn a little money, get some expo- sure. The commercials are going to be done anyway. Besides, it doesn't last long. A few years and images change, celebrity cools, it's over. It all evens out.

20   But it doesn't. We all lose, at least a little. We lose because you think I'm better than I am. Brighter than I am, kinder, more compassionate, capable of more things, as good at life as I am at the game. I'm not. Off the ice I struggle as you do, but off the ice you never see me, even when you think you do. I appear good at other things because I'm good at being a goalie; because I'm a celebrity; because there's always someone around to say I'm good. Because in the cozy glow of success, of good news, you want me to be good. It's my angle, and so long as I play well the angle won't change. I appear bright and articulate because I'm an athlete, and many athletes are not bright and articulate. "Like a dog's walking on his hind legs," as Dr. Johnson once put it, "it is not done well; but you are surprised to find it done at all."

21   But you don't believe that, just as I don't believe it about celebrities I don't know. They're taller, more talented, more compassionate. They glit- ter into cameras and microphones, give each other awards for talent and compassion, "great human beings" every one. Wet-eyed I applaud, and believe. And all of us lose. You, because you feel less worthy than you are. Me, because once, when I was twenty-three years old and trying to learn about myself, I wanted to believe I was, or soon would be, everything others said I was. Instead, having learned much and grown older, I feel co- conspirator to a fraud.

22   Professional athletes do exciting, sometimes courageous, sometimes ennobling things, as heroes do, but no more than you do. Blown up on a TV screen or a page, hyped by distance and imagination, we seem more heroic, but we're not. Our achievement seems grander, but it isn't. Our cause, our commitment, is no different from yours. We are no more than examples, metaphors, because we enter every home; we're models for the young because their world is small and we do what they do.

23   A few years ago, Joe McGinniss, author of *The Selling of the President, 1968*, wrote a book called *Heroes*. It sketches McGinniss's own tormented trail from being *the youngest*, to *the highly acclaimed*, to *the former* — all before he was thirty. At the same time, he ostensibly searches for the van- ished American hero. He talks to George McGovern and Teddy Kennedy, General William Westmoreland, John Glenn, Eugene McCarthy, author William Styron, playwright Arthur Miller — some of them heroes of his, all of them heroes to many.

24   But it's like chasing a rainbow. He finds that, as he gets closer, his heroes disappear. In homes and bars, on campaign trails, they're distinctly,

disappointingly normal. Not wonderfully, triumphantly, down-to-earth normal, but up-close, drinking-too-much, sweating, stinking, unheroically normal. And for heroes, normal isn't enough. We are allowed one image; everything must fit.

The Greeks gave their gods human imperfections. In the modern 25 hero, however, every flaw is a fatal flaw. It has only to be found, and it *will* be. Moving from celebrity to hero is like moving from a city to a small town. In a city, the camera's eye, though always present, is distant. In a small town, there isn't that distance. There's no place to hide.

"Whom the gods would destroy," Wilfrid Sheed wrote in *Transatlantic* 26 *Blues*, "they first oversell." Superficially created, superficially destroyed — for the hero, for the celebrity, it all evens out. Except a heavy price is paid along the way. We all lose again. You, because, saddened and hurt by heroes who turn out not to be heroes at all, you become cynical and stop believing. Me, because I'm in a box. What is my responsibility? Is it, as I'm often told, to be the hero that children think I am? Or is it to live what is real, to be something else?

Recently, a friend asked me to speak to his college seminar. Near the 27 end of two hours, we began to talk about many of these questions. A girl raised her hand. She said that a year or two earlier, on the Academy Awards, she had seen Charlton Heston receive an award for his "humanitarian" work. Heston had made the point, the girl said, that thousands of volunteers had done far more than he, that they deserved the award.

I asked the class what that story told them about Charlton Heston. 28 That he's even modest, they decided. A few of the students laughed; then, one by one, several others joined in.

READING

1. What does the opening anecdote tell us about Ken Dryden?

2. How does he define and classify celebrityhood in paragraphs four, five, and six?

3. What is a celebrity "persona" (paragraph five)? What does being "articulate" have to do with it? How does it relate to "image"?

4. Who is Dryden's audience? How does he engage and create his audience with the second person pronoun *you*, especially beginning paragraph sixteen?

5. How does he use personal pronouns — I, we, us, you — throughout, especially at the turn of his argument between paragraphs nineteen and twenty?

6. Do you accept the author's argument that we all lose in the game of celebrityhood? Consider the question in relation to other kinds of celebrities.

7. In Dryden's view, what is the relation between celebrities and heroes? Do you agree?

8. A crucial feature of his persuasive force is his presentation of himself in words, his creation of a persona through all the elements of the essay. How do you respond to this persona?

9. What is the more persuasive factor in the essay, his persona or his logic? Can you separate the two?

FROM READING TO WRITING

1. Consider a celebrity who exercised some sort of influence over your life. Try to evaluate whether this influence was positive or negative or both. Then, using your evaluation as an example, create an argument in which you take a position on celebrities in general.

Bruce R. Halladay

Bruce wrote "Mandatory Drug Testing in Canadian Sport" during his fourth year in university. His personal interest in sports— especially hockey, football, soccer, and squash—combined with the emotional letdown after Ben Johnson lost the gold medal in the 1988 Olympics, prompted Bruce to write this essay.

"While doing the research for this essay, I realized how much I care about the quality and fairness of North American sport," says Bruce. "... I felt I was voicing the opinion of the silent majority in expressing my concern for the future of sports."

Mandatory Drug Testing in Canadian Sport

TO MANY AMATEUR athletes, sporting competitions are a simple ₁ source of enjoyment. Events and contests are entered to compare oneself to others and to experience the thrill of competition. In recent years, however, the emphasis has been on winning, rather than on having fun. This situation has been especially prevalent at the highest level of amateur competition, the Olympic games. When the benefits of winning a gold medal include millions of dollars in endorsements, some people will do anything to win. One of the easiest methods to improve one's performance on the track or in the gym is the use of steroids. Clearly, mandatory drug testing of amateur athletes should be instituted in Canada because the use of steroids is destroying amateur sport in this country.

The days of the true amateur athlete are behind us. At one time, a ₂ professional athlete was someone who received money for participating in a particular sports activity. Such a wide definition might apply to almost everyone, including a 10-year-old hockey player whose father pays him a dollar for every goal he scores. At the other end of the spectrum are competitors in professional leagues who make millions of dollars every year, and millions more through advertising endorsements. Certainly, Olympic athletes have come to resemble professional sports figures more than individuals who compete solely for the thrill of participation. In many cases, these individuals are able to earn more money than many of the highest paid professionals. Something must be done to amateurize amateur sports.

3   North Americans are brought up to believe that winning is everything. This attitude runs through our economic and political situations and, above all, may be found in our sporting competitions. Steroids can provide the little extra that could make the difference between winning and losing; our attitude that winning is the only important consideration in competition has created the current abuse of steroids by athletes. The practice of drug abuse has been steadily increasing during the past several years, but the recent Olympic games in Seoul suffered the worst, and most public, record of abuse. For sports to remain credible, drug abuse by athletes must be stopped.

4   The first place to start changing the philosophy of winning at all costs that is undermining sports is at the Olympic games. The Olympic movement is finally seeing the light and beginning to open the games to all athletes, including some professionals. While the Olympics remain amateur, athletes will continue to cheat by using drugs, because the endorsements resulting from a gold medal performance are their only immediate means of income. Money and fame are two of the most powerful motivating forces, but there is a down side resulting from the excessive benefits that are generally received after winning a gold medal. Something must be done to moderate the financial rewards amateur athletes can receive; until this is done, however, drug testing will have to be the main deterrent stopping Olympic athletes from using drugs.

5   Canada has been among the most outspoken nations in its support for mandatory drug testing of amateur athletes. Despite the government's firm stand, Canada's image was tarnished more than any other nation's by the steroid scandal that emerged during the 1988 summer games. This embarrassment should only fuel the Canadian government's crusade to clean up the sporting world, starting in our own backyard. The government has taken the first step by initiating a public inquiry to determine the extent and the source of the problem, but the officials should be taking the opportunity to implement a drug testing policy for Canada's athletic representatives. A reasonable method might be to test all competitors during the first week of every month. According to a *Globe and Mail* report, most steroids stay in an individual's system for at least six weeks, which would make this sort of regular testing a serious deterrent. Such a testing policy would cover only those athletes who compete internationally, carrying Canada's colours. Other bodies, governing regional associations, would be responsible for implementing similar policies within their jurisdictions.

6   Less is said about the abuse of drugs at lower levels of competition, but likely abuse is as prevalent there as it is in the Olympic and professional ranks. Competition among athletes is just as fierce at the varsity level as it is at any other. The university level sports that will most likely produce professional athletes are hockey and football. In these sports, especially in

football, steroids are almost certainly being used. A student recruited straight out of high school is under tremendous pressure to excel, and using steroids to relieve some of this pressure, by making his work easier for him, appears to be a great solution to the problem. Compounding the situation, these kids are too young to realize fully the serious complications that can arise from using performance enhancing drugs. A similar program to that which was suggested earlier should be adopted by the Canadian Inter-Collegiate Athletic Union (CIAU). Such a policy would force Canada's young athletes to remain clean, and would create equal competition among players who are trying to reach the professional leagues.

It is more difficult, if not impossible, to institute a drug testing policy   7 to cover professional athletes. The National Football League (NFL) is attempting to enforce the policy it instituted some years ago, but it is having only moderate success. At this level, athletes are participating in their chosen profession, and any means at all of creating an advantage over others, even if it may lead to future disability or even death, is extremely difficult to resist. In spite of this, individuals who are known to be using dangerous substances should be required to participate in public awareness advertisements indicating that they are aware of the danger involved in their activities but do not care. Of course, this sort of campaign is not likely to be enough to deter other, younger athletes from exactly the same behaviour as they advance to the major leagues. While we must acknowledge the rights of individuals to use whatever legal means they choose to excel — and steroids are still not banned substances in some professional leagues — how can we tolerate the influence these sorts of "successful" athletes have on children?

The most important reason to implement drug testing is to protect   8 young children who will be our future athletes. Children tend to want to identify with the biggest, toughest, fastest athletes, and they try to emulate them in every way. Every kid in Canada wants to be a Ben Johnson or a Wayne Gretzky because they are the very best at what they do. During the Seoul Olympics, when Johnson was stripped of his medal, it was obvious that he did not suffer alone; we were all tremendously disappointed. However, this disappointment was undoubtedly felt most keenly by the children and young athletes for whom Ben Johnson represented the best they could possibly be.

Not only must we clean up competition because of the influence that   9 sports figures have on children, we must also eliminate the attitude that the use of steroids is acceptable. A very serious problem with performance enhancing drugs likely does not exist below the university level in Canada, but at the high school, and even junior high school, levels testing and education must begin. If school teams in the public education system were subjected to drug tests, a very strong impression would be made on all the athletes. At this level, any abuse would have to be dealt with severely to reinforce the absolute condemnation of any unfair competitive advantage, but of drugs in particular. In this way, measures to combat steroid abuse would already be implemented across the whole spectrum of amateur sports.

10   The use of banned substances by athletes at all levels is a serious problem, and the Canadian government is right to show a great deal of concern about steroid abuse. However, speeches, investigations, and inquiries are not enough; regular drug testing must be implemented, because the use of steroids affects everyone in our society, either directly or indirectly. Regular mandatory drug testing of all amateur athletes in this country would be very expensive, but it would be a very small price to pay in order to maintain credibility in the world of sports.

READING

1. What is Halladay's thesis? Where is it stated in the essay?

2. How does the author defend his statement that "the days of the true amateur athlete are behind us"?

3. Write an outline of this essay. What does the outline show about the essay's organization?

4. Are the author's arguments logical? If you perceive any flaws in his logic, which arguments are flawed and in what way?

5. What, according to the writer, is the most important reason to implement drug testing?

6. From what should young children be protected?

7. Reread paragraph four. Do you agree with the writer's statement that "while the Olympics remain amateur, athletes will continue to cheat by using drugs, because the endorsements resulting from a gold medal performance are their only immediate means of income"? Why or why not?

8. Why does Halladay think it is important to begin drug testing at the high school level? Do you agree with his assessment? Explain your answer.

FROM READING TO WRITING

1. Write an essay describing your reactions to the discovery of Ben Johnson's steroid use at the Seoul summer Olympics. Make notes on your initial response to the announcement and the development

or change in your feelings as more and more information was released to the public. Use your notes as the basis for your essay.

2. There is a Snoopy poster on which the caption reads, "If it doesn't matter whether you win or lose, why do they keep score?" A famous articulation of this sentiment is Green Bay Packer coach Vince Lombardi's motto: "Winning isn't everything. It's the only thing." Write an essay using either of these quotations as a focus. Decide on your opinion of the sentiment expressed, develop a clear thesis statement, and then write the argument essay supporting your point of view.

Gizelle Popradi

Gizelle is a first-generation Canadian, born to Hungarian parents in British Columbia. She has lived in Montreal for the past thirteen and a half years and attends Marianopolis College, taking Health Sciences. Although she enjoys the sciences, she says a part of her has always wanted to "be creative, and draw and write all of the time." In this essay she decided to "try a new tone," but still found that "this essay, like every other that I have worked on, reminds me about the value of editing and re-editing. Days, even weeks after I've written a piece, I always find a better word or a clearer way of phrasing a sentence."

Post–Saturday Morning Revelations

1   ORDINARILY, I am not among those who cry out against violence in the media, probably because I can still recall those glorious Saturday mornings that I would spend, eyes glued to the television screen and convulsed in giggles, watching some sadistic bird laugh in glee as giant anvils fell on a scrawny coyote or as this emaciated creature plummeted off Grand Canyonesque cliffs. Now, what I was witnessing every week was definitely violent by the standards of most people who even mildly oppose such things as nuclear arms, human sacrifice, and Brian Mulroney's re-election. Such cartoons should probably have given me the impression that bungee-cord diving without a cord was okay since I would be able to get right up again the next week, and do it over with minimal side effects. However, now that I am a mature young adult, I think that bungee-cord diving is ridiculous and have no desire to jump off any cliff, regardless of the good or bad consequences that might result from my demise. So basically my general attitude toward people who thought Saturday morning violence would scar me for life is: fie on you. Especially since I am not the only one who was subjected to such atrocities in my pre-being-smothered-by-homework-and-not-having-time-to-even-change-the-channel-with-the-remote days. And I think that my friends turned out just fine too, so: fie on you again.

2   Yet after suffering through a recent sobering experience that might have slapped me into reality, I am beginning to reconsider my opinion

and am wondering if I should start speaking out against violence in the media. Not too long ago, I found myself on my friend's porch, helping to give candy and UNICEF money to miniature hobgoblins, gangsters, and fleurs-de-lis (obviously a hot item to dress one's kid as in La Belle Province). As anyone can guess, it was Allhallows Eve, and I was trying to get into the Halloween spirit. I just might have been able to capture some of this spirit, had I not been so traumatized by the events of the evening. While innocently handing out goodies, I most certainly did not anticipate being accosted by a three-foot Rambo whose first and only words were "J'en veux beaucoup." Translation: "I want a lot." This demand threw me just a little, but I figured that the tyke was trying to be cute, so I gave him an extra bag of chips. Call me naïve and out of touch with today's youth, but I do not think that anything could have prepared me for what happened next. Rambo, obviously unsatisfied with my handout, pulled a plastic Uzi on me, said "blam, blam," and ran away with his fellow guerrillas, probably intent on terrorizing more unsuspecting CEGEP students. Safe to say that this traumatic experience probably scarred me more than any Saturday morning cartoon ever did.

Recovering from the initial shock of the event while discussing the 3 episode with my friends (who assured me that I was not in need of therapy), we agreed that his behaviour, and that of other children, probably stems from the violence that they are exposed to on television and in the movies. This violence not only shows them 101 ways to murder someone brutally but gives them the wrong ideas about the reality of guns and dangerous stunts. But even worse than that, the violence in the media that they are exposed to daily brainwashes everyone — not just children — into thinking that it is acceptable and expected. Parents never even give a second thought to little Bobby running around the house shooting everything in sight, including the cat, with a plastic bazooka. Twenty years ago he might have been using a garbage can lid and a wooden sword while playing with his friends, and 35 years ago he probably would have quietly been reading a comic book, because running around with a fake machine gun in 1957 was as rare as someone contracting the HIV virus. Violence has become more and more acceptable in our society, and that thought really disturbs me. I never have had any objection to watching someone get killed in a movie, but when some 6-year-old kid who has no idea who I am waves a fake gun at me for no reason, except for wanting more candy, I get really upset: not at the child, who has no idea that what he is doing is wrong, but at whatever showed him that waving a gun in someone's face was okay, in other words, the media.

On the other hand, I realize that my friends and I also watched vio- 4 lent cartoons and movies in our youth. I am now sure that they probably prompted us to do stupid things similar to waving toy guns at people, just as Rambo did. We have long since stopped doing that and have, I hope, turned into well adjusted people. ... But hey, wait a minute! Wasn't that my friend on Halloween, having a pretend gunfight with his little brother and stabbing a stuffed dummy while costumed as the grim reaper, his sole purpose being to scare little trick-or-treaters? Yes, it was. And I find it scary to think that the kids enjoyed watching his violence as much as he did.

5   None of this ever occurred to me until that little incarnation of Rambo stuck his toy Uzi in my face, proving just how commonplace and acceptable manifestations of violence have become. Now I have to admit that all those cartoons depicting coyotes being crushed by falling boulders did affect me. I may never have tried to throw myself off of a cliff, expecting to get up and walk away at the bottom, but I have built up a tolerance and a certain indifference toward violence, just as many others have. As more people regard it with apathy, violence will become more acceptable and more graphic, until perhaps its effects will one day be startlingly obvious. I really do not want to wait till that day comes to see something being done about it. Now is the time to speak out against violence in the media.

READING

1. How does Popradi attempt to strike a rapport with her audience in her first sentence? What audience is she addressing?

2. How would you characterize the tone of the first paragraph? How does this tone contribute to her presentation of her first position on the representation of violent acts on television?

3. What is her initial position?

4. How does the event described in paragraph two change her position?

5. In what ways does this change contribute to the development of her argument?

6. How does the author develop the connections between the incident and violence in the media in paragraph three?

7. What are the grounds for her changing her position in paragraphs four and five? Do you find these grounds sufficient?

8. Two basic ways to present an argument are to state your position at the beginning or at the end. Why do you think Popradi leaves the statement of her actual position until the end? Do you find this strategy effective in this case?

FROM READING TO WRITING

1. Popradi develops her argument not through formal logic, but through the use of narrative and example. Can you think of a similar example that changed your view of the media? Did this change allow you to see the positive or negative features of mass media? Write an essay in which you use that incident to demonstrate the power of the media.

2. What is the issue most important to you? Construct an argument in which you take a position on this issue. First, note all of the arguments you can make for your position. These arguments may include example, statistics, personal testimony, historical precedent, or formal logic. Then decide which arguments you will use and whether you will structure the argument by stating your position at the beginning or whether you will develop toward stating your position at the end. Create an outline, and write an essay arguing for your position.

Dan Zollmann

*In his last year of high school, Dan decided to study International
Development. This led him from Ottawa to West Africa to Quebec
City to Indonesia and then to Montreal and Vancouver. At university,
he graduated with a BA in Liberal Arts after studying everything from
Thomas Aquinas to quantum mechanics. Dan is now studying
screenplay writing and considering returning to university for Law or
Engineering studies.*

*"When writing this essay," Dan says, "I discovered how much
pleasure and satisfaction I derived from exploring phrasings,
restructuring sentences, and sounding out words. This, in turn, made
me realize that I find the act of writing to be fulfilling, independent of
its intellectual content. Certainly, to write well one must plan but, in
order to plan effectively, one must think and, as many have already
observed, writing is the most productive form of thinking."*

Illiterate like Me

1   MOST CANADIANS BELIEVE that something should be done to help
the illiterate. Yet other social issues often take precedence
when it comes to distributing tax dollars. If illiteracy were
simply an inconvenience suffered by a handful of Canadians, then the low
priority we accord to dealing with it would be justified because time and
money are finite, and we must allocate these scarce resources on the basis
of importance. However, illiteracy is not merely an inconvenience, nor
does it afflict only a few Canadians. Instead, it is nothing less than the
political, economic, and social alienation of a large number of individuals
from their society. As such, illiteracy is as urgent as any other social problem we face.

2   What is it really like to be illiterate? I do not know, nor will I ever be
capable of knowing, any more than I could know what it would be like to
be blind, or to be a paraplegic. Four years ago, however, I moved to
Quebec City to study French at Laval University, an experience that provided me with some insight into the reality of illiteracy. As someone who
had learned to speak French by ear, I knew the alphabet, could recognize
a few words, but had almost no practical experience reading and writing
French. In other words, at age 20 I joined the ranks of the illiterate.

How does an illiterate survive in a situation requiring a higher level of 3
literacy than most jobs in Canada require, namely, as a university student?
With great difficulty. Although in high school I had participated a great
deal in class discussions, in university I stopped offering my opinions
because I had no confidence in my understanding of the texts under
discussion. Always a good writer in high school, I now found myself incapable of finishing an essay exam question within the time limit, never
mind producing logical, concise answers. Even the basics of dealing with
the university's administration became a struggle: calendars, course
changes, registration forms, regulations, all were a complete mystery to
me. Sometimes the results were disastrous: for example, I accidentally
signed a form that forced me to spend hours the following year trying to
get readmitted to the university. Moreover, I had no idea how services
such as guidance, tutoring, or the ombudsman could help me deal with
these problems since I was incapable of fully comprehending my student
handbook.

Not only was attending university difficult, but the many problems 4
that literate people daily overcome suddenly became insurmountable. I
opened a bank account without even attempting to understand the form I
had to sign. My furnace broke down several times in the winter, yet I had
no idea to whom I should complain. Moreover, I was incapable of writing
a letter of complaint even if I had known where to send it. Although I
had some idea of the basics of written French, using it every day was
extraordinarily difficult because I knew that when I wrote in French I
made mistakes in grammar that most people stopped making after Grade
3. This embarrassed me to the point that I was afraid to put up an advertisement on the bulletin board to sell last term's textbooks, or to fill out a
job application, or to leave a note for someone on my apartment door, or
even to write down a phone message for a roommate. I became paralyzed
with fear when faced with the most trivial of daily tasks.

My inability to read or write also had a profound effect on the way I 5
related to my community. I constantly saw things around me that aroused
my anger, yet I was powerless to change them. For example, I wanted to
write a letter of complaint to the owners of the pulp mill that filled my
lungs with sulphur dioxide gas every time I passed by on the way to the
university, yet I knew that any letter I wrote would first be laughed at, and
then ignored. Since we tend to judge a person's intelligence by his or her
ability to write, how could I expect the owners of the pulp mill, or the
editors of a newspaper, to take seriously the complaint of someone who
appeared to be too ignorant to write beyond the primary school level?   6

Gradually, I became divorced from the world in which I lived. I voted
in the provincial elections, but I did not understand the brochures delivered to my apartment by the candidates. I occasionally bought *Le Devoir*

with the intention of reading it cover to cover, yet found myself incapable of following any article longer than a few paragraphs. Unable to read newspapers, I had to accept the second-hand reports of literate people around me. Unable to understand political debate, I judged on the basis of appearance, rather than issues. Incapable of communicating with my own community, I renounced all personal responsibility, hoping that others would write the letters, circulate the petitions, and lobby local officials. In short, I gave up, resigning myself to the frustrated yet passive existence of the alienated.

7   The comparison between my experiences in Quebec City and those of someone who is truly illiterate, however, can go only so far. After all, I was already literate in one language and was in Quebec by choice, not necessity. In contrast, the millions of Canadians who can neither read nor write either official language cannot simply pack their bags and return to their home province when they grow tired of their alienation. Moreover, it is quite possible that most of these people are not even aware of the extent to which they are isolated from society because they know no other existence, no other way of living. This, in turn, highlights the ultimate tragedy of illiteracy, namely that those who suffer from it are powerless to exert the political pressure necessary to change their situation.

8   Illiteracy is, therefore, more than merely a minor inconvenience. In Canada, and in all other Western societies, an inability to read and write means alienation from one's community and from one's country. At a political level, illiteracy makes a mockery of the democratic process by creating an oligarchy composed of an educated elite. At a personal level, illiteracy means subjection to economic and political marginalization; in short, the exploitation of one of the most vulnerable groups in society.

READING

1. What is Zollman's thesis? Is it explicit or implied?

2. What combination of rhetorical modes does he employ in writing his essay?

3. Do you think the author's comparison of his inability to function in French to that of an illiterate person is a fair one? Why or why not?

4. What parallels does he draw between his personal experience and that of the illiterate adult? What is the major difference between the two experiences?

5. Is paragraph five unified and coherent? Why or why not?

6. Select a paragraph that you think is a good example of unification and coherence. Explain your choice.

7. What is the author's most convincing argument for the urgency of educating the illiterate?

8. Does he effectively conclude his essay? Why or why not?

FROM READING TO WRITING

1. Think of a situation in which your inability to understand or speak another language created an embarrassing or humorous moment for you. Write a narrative essay in which you set the stage, describe the people involved, provide the dialogue, and explain the outcome of that moment.

2. What do you consider to be the societal problem most urgently in need of attention now? Write an essay explaining the reason for your choice and possible solutions.

CREDITS AND PERMISSIONS

GLOSSARY

Analogy: an extended, point-by-point comparison between two unlike things for the purpose of illustrating one of the compared things. Writers often use analogies when they are trying to explain unfamiliar or complicated concepts. For instance, a writer might explain the way that the human brain functions by comparing it to a computer.

Audience: the intended reader or readers of the writer's work. To communicate effectively with her or his audience, a writer must know the audience's expectations and level of understanding. The tone of the essay, the level of language used, and the amount of detail included will be determined by the needs of the audience.

Chronological Order: an ordering of time; events or ideas that are arranged chronologically are discussed in the order in which they occurred.

Coherence: the clear connection among the details and ideas of a piece of writing. In a coherent essay, one paragraph leads logically to the next; the subject is consistent throughout; and there are smooth, logical transitions made from point to point and from paragraph to paragraph.

Concrete and Abstract Language: Concrete language refers to particular objects, people, and events (the CN Tower, Pierre Trudeau, or the Olympics); abstract language refers to concepts and qualities (beauty, honour, courage).

Explicit Thesis: a thesis statement that is precisely and clearly expressed at the beginning or the end of an essay.

Figurative Language: highly descriptive language that is used in all types of essays. Metaphors, similes, and personification are examples of figurative language.

Implied Thesis: a thesis statement that is suggested by the content of the essay but is never directly stated. This type of thesis is often found in personal writing, where the writer is often more interested in suggesting meaning, rather than supporting an explicit argument.

Irony: a term generally applied to statements or events. An ironic statement says the opposite of what the speaker or writer means, or implies that something more is meant than is stated. An ironic sequence of events is one opposite to what might naturally be expected.

Prewriting: the exploratory stage of the writing process. It is usually the beginning of the process of clarifying one's topic and developing a thesis. Strategies such as free-writing and looping are often used during the prewriting stage.

Purpose: the aim of the essay. The purposes or aims of writing an essay can include expressing personal experience or ideas, informing, persuading readers to change their thinking about an issue, or inspiring readers to take action.

Recursive: returning repeatedly. We have used this adjective in this book to describe essay writing, which we suggest is rarely a straightforward, step-by-step process. Often the writer will find it necessary to repeat or return to earlier phases in the writing process. For instance, after deciding on a thesis statement, the writer might discover through research that the chosen thesis is no longer valid, and might have to go back to the prewriting stage and start again.

Satire: a form of humour, often biting, that ridicules foolish or vicious behaviour or ideas for the purpose of correcting them. The satirist uses exaggeration and irony to achieve her or his effect.

Thesis: the main idea or point that the writer wants to communicate to the reader in an essay. It is often expressed in a thesis statement, which can be explicit or implied. Either way, the thesis is the central idea that organizes the many smaller ideas and details of the essay.

Topic Sentence: the sentence that identifies the topic, or main idea, of a paragraph. It is usually found at or near the beginning of the paragraph.

Unity: oneness or wholeness. This quality is evident in a piece of writing if all ideas and details are connected to the central controlling idea of the essay. A unified essay deals with one idea at a time, focusses on one subject, and maintains one tone.

READER REPLY CARD

We are interested in your reaction to *Contest: Essays by Canadian Students*, Second Edition. You can help us to improve this book in future editions by completing this questionnaire.

1. What was your reason for using this book?

    ☐ university course   ☐ college course   ☐ continuing education course

    ☐ professional   ☐ personal   ☐ other _____
        development   interest   _____

2. If you are a student, please identify your school and the course in which you used this book.

3. Which chapters or parts of this book did you use?

4. Did you omit any chapters or parts? If so, which?

5. What did you like best about this book? What did you like least?

6. Please identify any topics you think should be added to future editions.

7. Please add any comments or suggestions.

8. May we contact you for further information?

    Name: _____

    Address: _____

    _____

    Phone: _____

(fold here and tape shut)

MAIL  POSTE

Canada Post Corporation / Société canadienne des postes

Postage paid
If mailed in Canada

Port payé
si posté au Canada

Business Reply

Réponse d'affaires

0116870399   01

0116870399-M8Z4X6-BR01

Heather McWhinney
Publisher, College Division
HARCOURT BRACE & COMPANY, CANADA INC.
55 HORNER AVENUE
TORONTO, ONTARIO
M8Z 9Z9